THE INTERNATIONAL ACCOUNTS

A Constructive Criticism of Methods used in Stating the Results of International Trade, Service, and Financial Operations

CLEONA LEWIS

Routledge
Taylor & Francis Group
LONDON AND NEW YORK

First published in 1927

This edition first published in 2014
by Routledge
4 Park Square, Milton Park, Abingdon, Oxon OX14 4RN
605 Third Avenue, New York, NY 10017

Routledge is an imprint of the Taylor & Francis Group, an informa business

British Library Cataloguing in Publication Data
A catalogue record for this book is available from the British Library

ISBN: 978-0-415-53081-1 (Set)
eISBN: 978-1-315-88628-2 (Set)
ISBN: 978-0-415-71789-2 (Volume 52) (hbk)
eISBN: 978-1-315-87101-1 (Volume 52)

THE INTERNATIONAL ACCOUNTS

A CONSTRUCTIVE CRITICISM OF METHODS USED IN STATING THE RESULTS OF INTERNATIONAL TRADE, SERVICE, AND FINANCIAL OPERATIONS

BY

CLEONA LEWIS

WITH THE AID OF THE COUNCIL AND STAFF OF THE INSTITUTE OF ECONOMICS

LONDON: GEORGE ALLEN & UNWIN, LTD.

RUSKIN HOUSE, 40 MUSEUM STREET, W.C. 1

Set up and printed.
Published July, 1927.

Printed in the United States of America by
J. J. LITTLE AND IVES COMPANY, NEW YORK

DIRECTOR'S PREFACE

As the sub-title of this volume indicates, the Institute of Economics has here undertaken a constructive criticism of the methods used in analyzing and presenting the results of the trade, service, and financial operations between any given country and the rest of the world. We have found from our studies of the international economic problems of various European countries that not only is the necessary information concerning international transactions far from complete, but that the international accounts have other serious shortcomings—owing to the fact that due consideration has never been given to the problem of suiting the accounts to the specific needs which they are intended to serve. In order to compile and present the data in a way that will best serve the varied purposes of those who make use of them, it is necessary to determine: (1) what purposes are to be served, (2) what information is required to meet these needs, and (3) how such information can best be presented in order to make it easily and clearly understood. It is expected that this technical study will lead to a great improvement in the methods of analyzing and presenting the international accounts.

The author of the book acknowledges with appreciation the assistance rendered by Constantine E. McGuire in the discussion of the Italian accounts, and by Leo Pasvolsky in the discussion of the accounts of Russia and the Danubian states. Likewise, the author desires to express grateful acknowledgment to Ray Ovid Hall (in charge of compiling the international accounts of the United States) for his detailed criticisms of the manuscript, and to Grosvenor M. Jones, Chief of the

Finance and Investment Division of the Department of Commerce, who carefully read and criticized the manuscript and wrote Appendix B.

HAROLD G. MOULTON,
Director.

Institute of Economics,
June, 1927.

CONTENTS

CHAPTER VI

CHAPTER VII

CHAPTER VIII

CHAPTER IX

APPENDICES

APPENDIX A

APPENDIX B

THE INTERNATIONAL ACCOUNTS

THE INTERNATIONAL ACCOUNTS

CHAPTER I

INTRODUCTION

The business transactions that take place between the people of different countries are of many kinds. In addition to trade in commodities across national frontiers there are exchanges of a less tangible sort. Services for which payment must be made are performed by the people of one country for the people of another; for example, British ships carry the ocean trade for many countries; German railways carry the transit trade for countries to the east; American banks and business houses execute commissions for foreign clients. People migrate from country to country—as tourists, as workers temporarily employed in a foreign country, or in search of new homes in foreign lands—with consequent transfers of funds. Borrowing and lending transactions of many kinds, involving payment of interest and dividends at later dates, take place across international boundaries.

In order to make real payment for the goods and services which they receive from foreigners, the people of a country must pay in goods and services. To pay in full they must be able to produce, and to sell abroad, goods and services of a total value equal to their requirements for foreign goods and services. If they cannot sell abroad enough to meet their foreign requirements, they will be forced either to obtain an extension of credit in foreign markets, or to cut down their purchases. On the other hand, if foreign demand for their

goods and services exceeds their foreign requirements, they will be forced to extend credit to foreigners or to refuse to sell in foreign markets as much as they otherwise might.

Few countries are in that happy state where foreign sales and foreign requirements are exactly equal. When everything is taken into account, the close of a year will show that some countries have gone deeper into debt to the outside world as a result of their transactions with foreigners during the year, or that their foreign investments and loans to foreigners stand at a lower figure than at the beginning of the year. Other countries will find that their claims against foreigners have increased, as a result of the year's operations, or that they have been able to scale down the volume of their foreign obligations.

Increases in foreign obligations involve increases in the amount of interest and dividends to be paid in the future—which, if not paid, will in their turn necessitate still further borrowings. And on the other hand, increases in foreign investments bring increased receipts of interest and dividends—which, if not taken in the form of goods and services, will be compounded year after year. In the long run these international movements of capital may have far-reaching effects on the exchange and currency, the trade and industry, and the general wealth and welfare of the countries concerned.

Statesmen, economists, and statisticians have long taken an interest in analyzing the causes and effects of these transfers of capital. In doing so they have found it necessary to have statistical measurements of the phenomena involved. They therefore have pieced together available data concerning the various classes of international transactions of particular countries. Their immediate purpose in these statistical inquiries has been, in some cases, to determine the net change in a country's foreign obligations or foreign investments that had resulted from a year's trade and service operations. Sometimes it has been to ascertain just what the standing of a particular country was, so far as international debts and invest-

ments were concerned. Sometimes the analyst has made an intensive study of a single class of international transactions, not taking account of other factors making for international movements of capital.

This work was well under way before the war. Some of the basic data required for the purpose were then, as now, regularly collected by government organizations—official trade statistics, for example, being collected by all countries. Other data have been secured from banks, shipping companies, security market reports, etc. These, while incomplete, give a basis for rough estimates of the various items to be taken into account. In a number of cases, also, where some particular problem called for a full survey of the international financial operations of a country, special commissions were officially appointed to investigate and report upon the question. In addition, private investigators and scientific societies not only gave attention to the task of compiling and analyzing the accounts of particular countries, but were also attempting to devise improved methods of collecting and using the required data.

These pre-war studies had been carried to a point where the international debt and investment position of most of the large trading nations of the world had been roughly determined. For example, it was known that Great Britain, France, and Germany were in the class of creditor nations; and that the United States, Russia, Argentina, and various others, were debtor nations. The net totals of their respective foreign investments and foreign obligations were also known in an approximate way.

The war and the economic readjustments that followed telescoped into a few years changes in the international financial position of various countries that would otherwise have extended over many decades, or might perhaps never have taken place. The war needs of European countries greatly increased their demand for goods from the United States,

and when peace was finally declared, there was no abrupt decline in the demand for American exports. To finance their war and post-war purchases, European countries were forced to liquidate the best of their foreign securities and to secure credit in one form or another in foreign markets. The result was a great reversal in the international debt and investment position of the United States and of many other countries.

The United States emerged from the war as a creditor, instead of a debtor, nation. The foreign obligations of her people and her industries had been greatly decreased, while claims against foreigners had been enormously increased. Great Britain had maintained her position as a strong creditor nation, but she had sacrificed some of her best foreign investments during the war and had replaced them by inter-ally loans of uncertain value. France had lost a large share of her investments through political upheavals and economic disorder in some of the countries that stood most in debt to her. Some of her best remaining investments had been sold abroad, and large foreign debts were accumulated in their stead. Germany had had almost all of her pre-war investments swept away and replaced by a large reparation debt which put a heavy burden upon the economic resources of the country and sent her seeking credit in foreign markets. Another group of states, already debtors in pre-war days, had increased the total of their debts during the war and the years immediately following. Russia had doubled her foreign debt—public and private. Italy also had incurred large additional obligations to foreigners. The countries of the Danubian basin had found themselves saddled with their respective shares of the pre-war Austro-Hungarian debts, in addition to the foreign obligations which they had contracted on their own account. Similar examples might be cited at length.

Much of the information collected before the war concerning the international financial position of these various countries has thus been rendered obsolete. Accounts compiled to show

their pre-war international income and outgo will no longer serve to indicate their ability "to pay their way" under these changed conditions. At the same time, of course, many new international problems have arisen, for whose solution revised data of this sort are almost indispensable. Of outstanding importance among these are the question of reparation claims and payments, and the question of inter-ally debts. And, with some lending countries turned borrowers, and some borrowers turned lenders, various old problems have taken on new meaning from the fact that they are now brought seriously to the attention of many people who had hitherto not been greatly concerned about them.

These perplexing questions have to do with both public and private affairs. The people of the United States, for example, with practically no experience in such matters, have been obliged to search out and examine the controlling factors which have to do with the making and receiving of international debt payments; they have had to find a basis for the settlement of foreign-government debts due to their government; and they have been expected to form opinions upon questions connected with Germany's reparation debt to the Allies. With little previous knowledge of foreign securities, they have been called upon to put their savings into loans floated by foreign governments, foreign municipalities, and foreign private enterprises. With little prior information at hand concerning their foreign customers, the exporters of the United States have had to pass upon requests for large extensions of credit.

Nor are the people of the United States peculiarly situated in this regard. For the people of Great Britain, France, and Italy, even more difficult questions impend. Germany, Austria, Hungary, in fact all of the late belligerents, must carry on their domestic affairs under the shadow of international trade and financial difficulties. Even the neutrals in the great war find that conditions have been greatly altered.

The various questions brought up for public and private

consideration in the United States, taking this country again as an example, have required the use of information concerning the international debt and credit position of the United States and also of the other countries involved. They have also required information concerning the current trade and financial transactions of this and other countries. The result has been a general quickening of interest in the compilation and interpretation of international trade and financial statistics. A great impetus has thus been given to the statistical work that was under way before the war.

As an outstanding development arising from all this, the governments of several countries have now begun the regular compilation and publication of their international accounts. Thus far this work has probably been carried farther in the United States than in any other country. The Department of Commerce of the United States has set in motion machinery for the collection of some data not hitherto available. Banks and business houses are furnishing information that has made it possible to estimate fairly closely several of the large items in the accounts. There is still a great deal to be done in the perfecting of this machinery, and in discovering new channels of information. But with the growing tendency on the part of the business world toward co-operation with the government, the actual collection of these data should gradually become less difficult. While the plan of work that the Department of Commerce has laid out for itself is much more ambitious than that which had been the rule before the war, it has on the whole been carried out with a fair degree of success.

A step recently taken by the League of Nations now promises that in time fairly complete financial and trade statistics of an international character will be generally available for most of the important countries of the world. Recognizing the need that exists for these data, the League regularly sends out questionnaires to all governments, asking for a statement concerning the international trade and financial transactions

of their respective countries. These statements are brought together and published in one of the memoranda issued annually by the League.

This work is undoubtedly of great importance, both for the present and the future. Projected on a world scale, as it is, it should contribute toward the development of better methods of obtaining and utilizing data needed for estimating the various items. Eventually, if the various countries can come to an agreement concerning a uniform technique to be adopted by all for the collection, compilation, and presentation of these accounts, it should be possible to check the statistical information set forth in the accounts of one country against that shown by the accounts of various other countries.

The reports which the League has brought together in its first three memoranda are, it is true, a somewhat heterogeneous lot as regards their content, their sources of data, and their methods. These, however, are matters that have not escaped the attention of the League statisticians. But since they must rely upon the governments of the different countries for the data that they present, they must make haste slowly. In some countries they find ready co-operation in their work. In other cases they find that they must convince skeptical officials of the value of collecting these data. Incidentally, it is worthy of note that, whereas most governments have for a long time recognized the advisability of keeping records of their budgetary income and expenditures, of the commodity trade, and of the agricultural and industrial production of their respective countries, many of them still regard the compilation of the international accounts as a matter too difficult, or too intangible, for them to undertake.

Despite the work now being done by various governmental groups, the recognized importance of the accounts, and the fact that they have long been a subject of inquiry and of interest, the technical equipment used in this particular section of the field of international finance is still in a very elementary

stage. There are still a great many teasing questions which arise concerning possible ways of obtaining data not now available, or concerning additional ways of utilizing existing information. The practical solution of these problems will depend in part upon the co-operation that business men will give to the government, and in part upon the co-operative action of the statisticians of different countries. There are also some very basic questions that still stand unanswered. Shortly before the war it was proposed that the purpose of the accounts should be defined, and that agreement should be reached concerning the content of the accounts. Such a definition of purpose would determine what data are needed for a complete statement of the accounts, and would help set the pattern in which the data should be brought together. Under the pressure of war work, however, the discussion was dropped. These questions of the purpose, content, and presentation of the accounts are the subject of the discussion which is to follow.

CHAPTER II

PURPOSES OF PRE-WAR INVESTIGATIONS

In post-war discussions of debt and reparation problems, great emphasis is put upon the importance of the international accounts in measuring a country's capacity to meet external obligations. This use has been so much stressed, in fact, that the idea of bringing together such data is sometimes thought to be an outgrowth of these discussions. This, however, is not the case. The accounts have been used, and are used, for a great many different purposes.

For the most part, pre-war studies of the international accounts were made to help solve some immediate problem faced by a particular country. As such questions arose, a technique had to be devised for collecting, compiling, and presenting the data required. Pioneering in the field was thus carried forward, now by one country, now by another. And gradually methods of work were developed and a body of data built up that made for rapid progress in the years just preceding the war. Beginning with the compilation of foreign trade figures in the early days when such figures were looked upon as indicators of international movements of gold and silver, they now include all classes of international financial data within their scope.

This chapter and the one which follows do not attempt to sketch the development of the accounts, however. They are rather intended to indicate the purposes that have motivated the more important studies that have been made in the United States and Canada, and in a number of the larger countries of Europe. While not pretending to be thoroughly exhaustive,

they will show the variety of problems that have called for the use of the accounts, the agencies interested in developing them, and the way in which earlier limitations are gradually being overcome.[1]

I. Currency Regulations

The currency question in its various aspects, has played an important rôle in the development of the international accounts. In fact this question, probably more than any other, has fostered and sustained interest in the collection, compilation, and presentation of data concerning the international trade and financial transactions of various countries.

The importance of foreign trade data was greatly emphasized by the mercantilists in their discussions of the nation's gold supply. In their efforts to conserve the national supply of gold and silver, they had need for a tool that would help them determine what the actual course of affairs was. Commodity import and export data were recognized as being of undoubted importance in this connection, and the relative ease with which they could be obtained recommended their collection and use. In view of the fact that guards had long been required along national frontiers for purposes of protection, the work of recording foreign trade movements could be handled with comparatively little added expense. Moreover, trade statistics are a natural by-product of customs duties; and the exaction of customs duties, already a practice of long standing, was strongly endorsed by the mercantilist program.

The relationship between international trade and national holdings of the precious metals was, of course, much exaggerated by the early mercantilists who pretty generally accepted

[1] We are leaving out of consideration here those studies which deal only with a single source of income or outgo, for example, studies dealing only with the income from shipping, from insurance, or from emigrants' remittances. The reason for this will be explained by the analysis which follows in Chapters IV and V.

the doctrine that an excess of commodity imports over exports necessarily involved a drain upon the country's gold supply. Data purporting to show gold movements were given little credence, for it was known that gold was being smuggled from country to country in considerable quantities. By the middle of the seventeenth century, British writers occasionally took note of the likeness that exists between commodity exports and the services rendered to foreigners by those engaged in shipping and marine insurance.[2] But in the main, no mention was made of these and other "service items" and even when mentioned, no statistical measurement for them was attempted. It was not until the beginning of the eighteenth century that rough methods began to be devised for determining the foreign purchasing power that a country might gain from these sources.

As a rule they also failed to take account of the inter-relationship existing between foreign loans and the currency problem. The practice of borrowing and lending abroad had long been a common one, however. As early as the thirteenth century, in fact, the rulers of Western Europe had been frequent borrowers from foreigners. But it was not until the practice of borrowing and lending abroad—on both public and private account—became more widely prevalent in the eighteenth and nineteenth centuries, that the necessity for assembling data concerning foreign loans and borrowings gradually became apparent.

After the Napoleonic wars, Britain's currency difficulties were made the subject of a comprehensive investigation. This is one of the earliest instances where international trade and financial data were both brought together in the same inquiry. Specie

[2] See for example Mun, Thomas, *England's Treasure by Foreign Trade* (1664), pp. 15 and 24; and *The Economic Writings of Sir William Petty*, brought together and edited by C. H. Hull (1899), p. 16. It should be noted here that the collection of trade figures in Great Britain dates back to the middle of the seventeenth century. In France, the orderly compilation of trade data began in 1827, but such information was collected in a less systematic way many years before.

payments had been suspended by the Bank of England since 1797, and although the Bullion Report of 1810 had urged resumption of "cash payments," the currency was, in 1819, still on an inconvertible basis. The question of resumption was, therefore, again taken up for consideration in 1819 by a parliamentary committee which, in the course of its investigation, endeavored to obtain a rough measure of the gold and silver movements of Great Britain. As the members of the committee phrased it, they wanted to determine the "balance of payments of the country"—a term which they used to mean the net amount of specie passing to or from Great Britain in settlement of a year's international transactions.

The items included in this inquiry were commodity trade, interest income and outgo, and the purchase or sale of new securities; the balancing item, as we have said, being accepted as a measure of the net movement of specie. For bringing together this information, the committee held extensive hearings where witness after witness was called to testify. Data concerning British investments in other countries, for example, were secured by questioning members of banking firms engaged in foreign borrowing and lending transactions. On this point the main source of information used by the several witnesses was the records of their respective firms with regard to interest and dividends received for the account of British investors.[3] As might be expected the various estimates thus furnished were not entirely in agreement, but they were close enough to meet the needs of the committee.

Currency conditions in the United States during the nineteenth century frequently focused attention upon the international accounts. Following the financial crisis of July, 1893, specie was drained from the country at such a rate that the situation became acute. It was seriously questioned whether the gold standard could be much longer maintained. Eventu-

[3] *Reports* from the Commons' Committee on Resumption of Cash Payments (Parl. Papers 1819, III), pp. 13-14 and 114.

ally a syndicate of bankers undertook to check this outflow of gold. While they were struggling with this task an article appeared in the *Forum* estimating that the country was borrowing from foreigners something like an annual amount of 350 million dollars.[4] This sum, according to the article, was required each year to meet the deficiency on account of excess imports of commodities, interest due on previous borrowings, expenditures of tourists, and shipping charges payable to foreigners. The estimate was very disturbing. To calm the fears of foreign investors—who had already begun withdrawing their funds from the country—the *Commercial and Financial Chronicle* made an independent study of the interest and dividends item in the account. On the basis of data obtained from bankers handling most of the security transactions between the United States and Europe, the *Chronicle* vigorously disputed the *Forum* estimate for this item, and stoutly maintained that the situation as a whole was not as bad as it had been painted.[5]

Fifteen years later a much more comprehensive study of the international accounts of the United States, by Sir George Paish, was published as part of the Report of the National Monetary Commission.[6] Again the question at issue was the maintenance of an adequate gold supply; a question which, as Paish saw it, would be answered in terms of the international credit position of the country. As he phrased it: "In these days it may be said that the movements of gold and silver are brought about not so much by trade balances as by the currency and banking needs of the various countries. If a country desires to obtain gold, it has no difficulty in buying

[4] *The Forum*, February, 1895, pp. 647-651.

[5] *Commercial and Financial Chronicle*, Vol. LX, 1895, pp. 542 and 631. Following the publication of the first of these articles, Mr. Heidelbach, the writer of the *Forum* article, published an open letter in the *Chronicle* in which he revised his earlier estimate; *ibid.*, p. 585.

[6] Senate Document No. 579, 61st Congress, 2d Session (1910), pp. 153-213.

it, provided that its credit is good."[7] His credit analysis takes up the question of the outstanding foreign debts of the country, the general purpose for which these debts have been contracted, and a broad classification of the total. Finally, he presents a statement of the current international transactions of the country, including foreign trade, interest, tourist trade, remittances to friends, and freight; showing, by a comparison of total outgo with total income, the rate at which new debts were then being contracted.

During the nineties of the past century, Russia's international accounts were examined for the purpose of testing proposed currency reforms. The government was making its final preparations for placing the Russian currency on a gold basis—an ambition realized in 1897. The Ministry of Finance was, therefore, anxious to know how far the actual state of the country's international financial accounts would permit the safeguarding of the metallic stocks accumulated for the maintenance of a gold currency.

Studies made for this purpose were concerned not only with such items as the movement of interest and dividends on governmental and private loans, tourist expenditures, etc., but serious efforts were made to check the accuracy of official trade statistics.[8] The best work on this last subject (V. I. Pokrovsky's "The Stability of the Russian Balance of Trade," St. Petersburg, 1896) attempts to demonstrate, for example, that the Russian excess of imports over exports during the period 1890-1895 was at least 13 per cent greater than indicated by the official figures, owing to the fact that Russian customs authorities were more precise in the evaluation of imports than of exports.

Several years later a similar problem enlisted the attention of Austrian economists. This was approximately at the turn of

[7] Senate Document No. 579, 61st Congress, 2d Session (1910), p. 164.

[8] See Ozerov, Ivan, *Osnovy finansovoy Nauki* (Elements of Financial Science), Vol. II, Moscow, 1908.

the century, when the Austro-Hungarian Monarchy was engaged in the task of establishing the gold standard. Serious efforts were made—notably by Dr. Ignaz Gruber—to evaluate the various items making up that country's international accounts, and thus to estimate the probable adequacy of the gold reserves.[9]

II. Testing Proposed Tax Measures

Taxation questions of immediate interest have, in many instances, motivated the compilation of foreign debt and investment data. Sometimes the purpose in hand was answered by a rough estimate of the capital value of a single large class of debts or investments. Sometimes it seemed desirable that the inquiry should include all available information on the international debt and investment position of a country, and on its current income or outgo on this account.

British history furnishes the somewhat exceptional case of an inquiry made to forecast the results of a proposed capital levy. In 1815, with the Napoleonic wars just ended, Great Britain was proposing to restore her shattered finances by a tax on capital. To determine the amount of capital subject to a tax of this kind, it was necessary to know the extent to which British securities were held by foreigners—securities so held not being taxable in Great Britain. Government tax records furnished a basis for a rough estimate of foreign holdings of government securities, and this estimate was deemed satisfactory for the purpose for which required.[10]

[9] *Bulletin de l'Institut international de Statistique,* 1905, Vol. XV, Part II, pp. 113-198.

[10] Acworth, A. W., *Financial Reconstruction in England, 1815-1822,* p. 58. The estimate was based on the exemptions claimed in connection with the tax on dividends under the property tax account. Estimates of total foreign investments in British securities—also based on these tax data—are given for the years 1762, 1806, and 1810-1818, by William Fairman in *An Account of the Public Funds,* 7th ed., 1824, p. 231.

The history of the United States shows certain other tax problems that have required the collection of foreign debt data. In 1843 the efforts of the people to lighten the pressure of direct taxes in the several states of the Union brought the question of foreign debts to the attention of Congress. The states were still suffering from the effects of the panic of 1837, and many of them were operating under the heavy burden of recently contracted debts. Hoping to ease the situation, people from a number of the states and territories submitted memorials to Congress asking that the national government shoulder these debts, substituting its own "stock" for outstanding state securities.[11] These petitions, as a matter of course, led to a Congressional investigation, from which it developed that most of the debts in question were owed to foreigners. The Committee in charge of the investigation reported in favor of the memoralists, shifting their ground, however, from the question of taxation to that of currency. A foreign debt, they argued, is always more onerous than a domestic debt. But if this foreign debt were assumed by the national government—incidentally, at a lower rate of interest—and if interest were made payable at the United States Treasury, the result would be that a large part of the interest paid would find its way to Europe in the form of cotton, tobacco, and other surplus domestic products, thus conserving the country's slender stock of gold. For their data they apparently relied upon their general knowledge of conditions and upon readily available information, rather than upon an original, first-hand investigation.[12]

The rapid development of the country in succeeding years entailed further borrowing from Europe, and in 1853 the question of foreign debts was again brought before Congress. It was argued by Senator Brodhead that:

[11] According to L. H. Jenks, this movement was started by Baring Brothers when it became apparent that a number of the states would be unable to meet their debts. *The Migration of British Capital to 1875*, pp. 105-106.

[12] House Report 296, 27th Congress, 3d Session, March 2, 1843.

In view of the speculative spirit of the country and the number of state and corporation bonds sold in Europe, it seems impossible to have anything like stability in our revenue laws. It seems to be impossible to make tariff laws which will stand against the ways of Providence, the course of commerce and trade, and the influence of the speculating mania. What is protection one year is none the next, and what is a revenue standard one year is none the next.

To show the full effect upon the country of its rapidly accumulating foreign debts, he presented estimates of the net outgo of the United States on account of the import surplus of commodities, interest on securities held abroad, expenditures of American tourists abroad, expenditures of the foreign diplomatic service, and of the navy in foreign stations, the indemnity paid to Mexico, and the remittances of immigrants to their friends and relatives abroad. From this he deducted the estimated amount of gold and silver brought into the country by immigrants, and net exports of gold and silver. The balancing item he took to be the net increase in foreign indebtedness, pointing out that, in the future, interest on this amount would enter into the account.

Urging that Congress should have full information concerning the foreign indebtedness of the country, he presented a resolution to the Senate directing the Secretary of the Treasury to inquire and report concerning "The aggregate amount of Federal, State, city, county, railroad, canal, and other corporation bonds, stocks, or other evidence of debt held in Europe, and other foreign countries, on the 30th June, 1853, specifying separately so far as can be ascertained, the amount of each of the above description of bonds and stocks."[13] The resolu-

[13] Appendix to the *Congressional Globe,* 32d Congress, 3d Session, (1853), pp. 309-311. Anxiety concerning these debts was now greater than anxiety concerning the gold supply, a point brought out by Seward's comments upon Brodhead's resolution: "I entirely agree . . . that, instead of sending paper to England, we had better send gold; and instead

tion having been adopted, the Treasury sent questionnaires on the subject to all the states. Data compiled from replies filed by the states, were revised and corrected by the firm of Winslow, Lanier and Company, and published by the Treasury in a report by the Secretary dated March 2, 1854.[14]

Again in 1869 the taxation question was responsible for an inquiry into the foreign debt position of the United States. From the summer of 1861 until the summer of 1865, the financing of the Civil War had resulted in steadily increasing taxes. In 1866, the year in which these taxes reached their highest limit, a Special Commissioner of the Revenue, David A. Wells, was appointed to study and report upon questions of taxation, trade, industry, and commerce. The fourth annual report of this officer states that the burden of taxation in the United States was then (1869) greater than in Great Britain, for, while the amount of revenue collected in the two countries was practically equal, the United States had the smaller accumulation of national wealth. The report continues with some detailed recommendations for tax revisions.

The point of interest here is that in connection with his estimate of the national wealth and national income of the country, the Commissioner made a very careful survey of all classes of foreign debts, basing the estimates that he gave upon first-hand information obtained from banks, railway companies, and from state and Federal authorities. Wells, like Brodhead, was interested in showing by what means and at what rate the debts were increasing. He therefore appended to his debt statement estimates showing the international income and outgo of the United States for the fiscal year 1868-69 from trade, interest, shipping, and the tourist trade; the net excess of

of sending either, we had better send whatever we can produce by cultivating the soil, or by manufacturing its products."

[14] Senate Executive Document, No. 42, 33d Congress, 1st Session. For excerpts from this report, see Appendix A, pp. 137-140.

outgo indicating the net increase in the debt.[15] His statement of these accounts is very interesting for its originality of method and of material, and compares very favorably with work of a similar character that was done a few years later in Great Britain.

III. Ascertaining Volume and Trend of Foreign Assets

To whom credit should be given for first recognizing the reserve strength represented by foreign investments and of showing their bearing upon a country's ability to buy in foreign markets or to meet foreign obligations is not a matter of particular importance. Suffice it to say that the first British investments abroad on anything like a large scale—following the close of the Napoleonic wars—was watched with some uneasiness in Great Britain.[16] By the middle of the nineteenth century, however, the importance of this class of national wealth and the factors making for its growth or decline were becoming pretty generally recognized. Some of the most important studies of the international accounts were made as a result of uneasiness lest this class of national wealth was being consumed through the extravagant purchase of foreign commodities.

In 1874 a French document appeared which gave dramatic emphasis to the economic importance of foreign investments. Léon Say, together with other members of the committee

[15] Wells, David A., *Report of the Special Commissioner of the Revenue, 1869*, House of Representatives, Executive Document No. 27, 41st Congress, 2d Session, pp. XXVI-XXXI, and LXV. For excerpts from this report see Appendix A, pp. 145-150.

[16] An indication of this is to be found in the *Hearings* of the Commons' Committee of 1819, referred to on pages 11-12. The question is also discussed at some length by a British writer of the day, John Marshall, who admits that the immediate effect of these loans was good, but was uneasy concerning their long-run consequences. John Marshall, *Statistics of the British Empire*, 1833, pp. 120 a-b. See also Jenks, L. H., *The Migration of British Capital to 1875.*

appointed to investigate the means employed by France in meeting the German indemnity, included in his report a rough summary of the international trade and financial transactions of France during the indemnity period.[17] Foreign securities to a total of about two billion francs, according to Say, were sacrificed to provide a part of the funds required, while interest received on foreign securities provided an additional means of payment. Commodity and specie imports and exports and income from tourist expenditures are also included in the account. But because he failed to give information concerning the extent to which foreigners bought up the domestic bonds issued by the French Government during the war, he fell somewhat short of accomplishing his purpose, for he thus made it impossible for his reader to determine from this report the full effect of the war on the international financial position of the country.[18] Despite this omission, however, Say's set of accounts is more inclusive than any published for France theretofore, or for many years to come.

Numerous investigations have been made to determine whether or not Britain's imports were being produced at the sacrifice of her foreign investments. The first of these was published in the sixties of the past century. Since then this purpose, probably more than any other, has been the motivating force in British investigations in this field. Some of the studies made during the sixties, seventies, and early eighties are of particular interest, for it was during this period that methods of estimating the various income and outgo items in the British accounts were being developed.

Among these, and important from the viewpoint of methodology, is an article published in the (London) *Economist,*

[17] Say, Léon, *Rapport sur le paiement de l'indemnité de guerre,* 1874, pp. 70-71.

[18] It may be added that many later writers who have based their calculations on Say's works have also overlooked the foreign debt contracted at this time, the result being that they have consistently overestimated the net amount of the interest income of France for later years.

December 8, 1877, by A. D. McKay, a merchant of Liverpool. This was written in reply to an earlier article, in the same paper, in which commodity import and export data had been used to show that the country was using up its earlier foreign investments. McKay showed that the official figure for imports was too large, because it included freight charges, mostly payable to British ship-owners, and a variety of landing and warehousing charges which were also payable to people in Great Britain. On the other hand, he showed that the figure for exports was too small because it was exclusive of the freight charges which foreigners were paying to British ship-owners, and of insurance charges, bankers' commissions, etc., most of which were collected from foreigners by people in Great Britain.[19] Drawing up a series of estimates for the 19-year period, 1858-1876, he showed that when allowance was made for these misstatements in the figures, the result was to reduce the import surplus for the period from a total of 1,193 million pounds sterling to 23 millions.[20] McKay thus made allowance for certain facts that previously had not been taken account of in British investigations. But on the other hand he failed to bring interest and dividends into the reckoning, although he refers to this item; and, as a matter of fact, it had been subject to rough statistical measurement for more than a half century.[21]

In the following March the great English statistician, Sir

[19] In short, British imports were valued on a c.i.f. basis; exports, f.o.b.; a custom that has been followed down to the present time. This had also been pointed out by Stephen Bourne in a study in which he presents a less complete set of accounts. *Journal of the Royal Statistical Society,* March, 1877, pp. 19-34. For excerpts from McKay's letter, see Appendix A, pp. 151-154.

[20] The main facts in this argument are reproduced by W. Newmarch in the *Journal of the Royal Statistical Society* for June, 1878.

[21] See discussion of the Commons Committee of 1819, pp. 11-12 of this book. Notice also that American writers had been including estimates for certain of these items in their studies of the accounts—although the methods they used were not the methods employed by McKay.

Robert Giffen, read a paper at the meeting of the Royal Statistical Society, stating that his purpose was to measure the recent accumulations of capital in Great Britain, and, incidentally, to determine the total wealth and "margin of taxation" of the country.[22] This inquiry, of course, necessitated a study of the foreign investments of the country as well as of domestic accumulations of capital,[23] and when the meeting was thrown open for discussion it was on this one item that attention was centered. "Whether we are eating up our capital abroad or not," said one of the speakers, Stephen Bourne, harking back to the topic of the day, "depends upon whether the income accruing to us is equivalent to the balance we have to pay on the settlements of our accounts." This brought from the next speaker, Mr. Mundella, M.P., the assurance "that certain kinds of (foreign) investments are still being made at an increased ratio."[24] In support of this statement he practically summarized the line of argument taken by McKay, although he, unlike McKay, included the interest and dividends item in his statement.

Four years later, Giffen made a more inclusive study of the British accounts, specifically setting out to show that Great Britain was not consuming her foreign capital. In this paper he gave special attention to the calculation of income from shipping, commissions, and insurance; presenting several methods of estimating which have been little improved

[22] *Journal of the Royal Statistical Society,* March, 1878. By the phrase, "margin of taxation," Giffen means the amount which the nation might have paid in taxes at the time he was writing and still have remained "as rich individually as it was ten years before," pp. 19-20.

[23] As a basis for this estimate, Giffen made use of the Inland Revenue Reports on the income tax assessments; a method that had been suggested by an anonymous writer in the (London) *Economist,* December 12 and 19, 1863 (articles reproduced in the *Journal of the Royal Statistical Society,* March, 1864, pp. 118-27). This method had also been used by Mr. Dudley Baxter in a paper prepared for the Society in 1868.

[24] *Journal of the Royal Statistical Society,* March, 1878, pp. 34 and 36-37.

upon since his time. He also gave a rough estimate of the interest item, basing it upon current information and general impressions. For the rest of the problem he said:

I do not propose to go farther into this question of the balance of indebtedness in the international transactions for the United Kingdom. To complete it would require an elaborate investigation of the magnitude of private investments, while such points as the expenditure of British citizens abroad, and the expenditure by foreigners in this country, and the minor movements of international capital in connection with exchange operations, would all require to be considered. . . . I shall be quite content if I have established to your satisfaction (1) that the question to be investigated is not that of the diminution, but of the increase, of our investments abroad . . . and (2) that, whatever may be our conclusions on this point, the import and export figures themselves are only a small part of the question, and that the use of these figures by some writers as if they were the whole, is only to be excused, if it is excusable, on the score of ignorance of the nature of statistics and the necessary conditions of dealing with them.[25]

Three comprehensive reports by Sir George Paish—two prepared for the Royal Statistical Society and one for the Manchester Statistical Society—bring the data with regard to British foreign investments down to the eve of the war. The point of view taken by Paish in these inquiries is slightly different from that of Giffen, although the two are closely related. Both of them saw in these investments a class of national wealth from which Britain derives an important share of her national income. But whereas Giffen was interested in finding whether the total invested abroad was increasing or decreasing, Paish's problem narrowed down to the determination of the actual amount of this total, and the various classes into which it divides. The discussion, following the presentation of the papers, tied back very closely to Giffen's work. For

[25] *Journal of the Royal Statistical Society*, March, 1882, p. 223. Brought down to date in 1899. *ibid.*, March, 1899.

example, an estimate of the international income available for investment abroad was presented by Edgar Crammond, who based his estimates upon those which Giffen had made.[26]

IV. Shedding Light on Economic Developments

In many cases the international accounts have been analyzed to show the effect of a country's borrowing and lending operations upon its economic development. This view of the question is much broader than that of simply determining how much of the national wealth of a lending country is represented by foreign investments, or to what extent the national wealth of a borrowing country is offset by its foreign debts. Two official inquiries, however, that set out to show the effects of foreign loans upon some particular phase of the economic life of the country in question, narrowed down in their published form to nothing more than statements concerning the amount of the investments themselves. On the other hand, the published results of certain other investigations discuss fully the larger questions involved.

Two German investigations relate the question of foreign investments to that of the economic development of the country. In 1897 an official study of Germany's foreign investments was included in a report presented to the Reichstag in connection with a bill for enlarging the German fleet. The investment data thus brought together are quite inadequate, amounting to nothing more than a collection of stock exchange

[26] Journal of the Royal Statistical Society, September, 1909, pp. 465-95; and January, 1911, pp. 167-200. *Transactions* of the Manchester Statistical Society, February, 1914 (Session 1913-14), also published as a supplement to the *Statist* for February 14, 1914. In this third paper, Paish relates the question of international investments with that of the increase in the cost of living in the world.

From the point of view of methodology, Paish's work is important. Like Giffen, he made use of the Inland Revenue Reports on the income tax assessments, but he supplemented these by a study of the reports of companies operating abroad, examining "the reports of as many of these companies as it is possible for a private person to secure."

information concerning certain placements, and a number of earlier estimates that had been made by various German scholars.[27]

Eight years later the whole report, including the section on foreign investments, was revised and expanded, and came out as a special report by the German Marine Office. The revision of the foreign investment section was made on the basis of data collected in answer to questionnaires that had been sent out to German consuls and diplomatic agents abroad. But again this section of the report is unsatisfactory. It makes no attempt at a complete statistical summary of the reports from the various officials, such a summary, in fact, being practically impossible since some of the replies had been couched in very general terms. Neither in this revised form nor in the original is there any discussion of the effects of foreign investments upon the employment of German tonnage, or upon German trade and industry.[28]

In 1913 an estimate of German foreign holdings was made in connection with a general study of the national wealth and national income of the country. This first appeared in a volume published to commemorate the twenty-fifth year of the Kaiser's reign, a volume composed of a number of large sections contributed by leading German writers of the day. One section of three chapters on the subject of Germany's economic progress from 1888 to 1913 was written by Dr. Karl Helfferich. The last chapter of the three was devoted by Helfferich to a discussion of national wealth and national

[27] *Stenographische Berichte der Verhandlungen des Reichstages, 9 Legislaturperiode, V Session, 1897-8. Anlageband I Aktenstuck, 5,* pp. 11-90.

[28] *Die Entwicklung der deutschen Seeinteressen im letzten Jahrzehnt, Sonderheft zur Marine-Rundschau,* 1905. As appendices to this volume the government published in full the French report of 1902, referred to two paragraphs below, and a British study on foreign investments entitled "Some Aspects of National Finance," by Edgar Speyer, originally published in the *Report* of the Institute of Bankers, June 7, 1900.

income, a discussion that would have been incomplete had he not included, as he did, estimates of the income derived from foreign investments and of the capital amount of these investments. This use of the data is of particular interest, for too often it is not seen that foreign investments and foreign debts must be considered in estimating a country's national wealth and income. From the point of view of methodology the estimate is of negligible importance, for apparently it is nothing more than a rough guess based upon a number of earlier estimates. Because of Helfferich's intimate knowledge of German financial affairs, however, it has been widely accepted and quoted. And since the war it has been taken as a starting point for many inquiries attempting to disclose what remnant of foreign holdings was still left to Germany.[29]

The much-quoted official survey of French investments abroad, apparently was due to anxiety lest these should adversely affect domestic enterprises.[30] This was made in 1902, at a time when there were many people in France who felt that too much capital was being invested abroad and too little in industrial and commercial enterprises at home. The investigation was carried through under the direction of the Minister of Foreign Affairs, who required the French diplomatic agents and consuls abroad to send in answers to a questionnaire regarding French investments in their districts. The results of this inquiry were published by the government with a colorless introduction stating that it would be of interest to know the total amount of French capital invested abroad, its geographi-

[29] Helfferich, Karl, *Germany's Economic Progress and National Wealth, 1888-1913* (Translation published by the Germanistic Society of America), particularly pp. 112-113. Incidentally, it may be pointed out that Helfferich shows what part of the national income was devoted to public purposes, what part to private consumption, and what part was added annually to the national wealth of Germany.

[30] "Lysis's" book, *Contre l'oligarchie financière en France,* gives some idea of the state of the public mind on this question.

cal distribution and the general character of the investments.[31]

Foreign capital has played a large part in the development of Canadian resources. Here we find an explanation for the Canadian study entitled "Capital Investments in Canada," with a sub-title which reads, "Some facts and figures respecting one of the most attractive investment fields in the world."[32] In his introductory note the author says that he has spared no pains to make the book "of commanding value and accuracy to bankers, financiers, investors, industrial, and commercial interests." Starting with the assumption that the future development of the country would depend in large measure upon capital secured from other countries, he is interested in helping to secure this capital—rather than in an analysis of the economic effects of these loans.

Of much broader scope and purpose than any of the inquiries thus far mentioned in this section, is the official report on the *Rise in Prices and the Cost of Living in Canada,* published by the Canadian government in 1915. A general request from the people of Canada for an investigation into the increase in the cost of living in the Dominion had resulted in the appointment of a Commission to study this question. Presented to the Canadian Prime Minister on August 1, 1914, the report of this Commission was published in two large volumes. The second volume, prepared under the direction of R. H. Coats,

[31] Published in the *Journal Officiel* for Sept. 25, 1902, and in the *Bulletin de Statistique et de Législation Comparée,* October, 1902, pp. 450-483. A good résumé was published in the *Journal of the Royal Statistical Society,* December, 1903, p. 729; and a critical analysis, by P. Leroy-Beaulieu, was published in *l'Economiste Français,* Oct. 4, 1902, pp. 449-51. For the résumé published in the *Journal of the Royal Statistical Society,* see Appendix A, pp. 142-143.

[32] By Fred W. Field. Published first as a series of articles in the *Monetary Times.* The first of these appeared in 1909, the last in 1911, and the book in which they are brought together is dated September, 1911.

Dominion Statistician, devotes one long chapter to the growth and distribution of capital from 1900 to 1914, and its relation to the rise in prices. The aggregate amount of foreign capital borrowed by Canada is calculated,[33] and the uses made of it are traced by the help of earlier studies and by reference to official Canadian statistics of various kinds. Data on these various subjects, together with data on labor, production, distribution, and savings, are summarized in a large final section entitled "Cost of Living and its Economic Causes."

An English study published just before the war raises the whole question of the economic effects of international transfers of capital. The author, C. K. Hobson, sees in the international accounts of a country a method of obtaining information concerning the growth of its foreign investments. And of foreign investments, he says:

> . . . The phenomenon is not merely economic in nature; it has profound ethical and moral significance. Seeds of the material civilization of Western Europe are being scattered more and more thickly over the most distant parts of the world, particles of energy which are destined to exert an influence of increasing potence upon human life and thought.
>
> . . . In forming an opinion as to whether foreign investment is good or bad—as to how far it should be encouraged or discouraged—it is essential to ascertain as definitely as possible whether or not the movement increases the economic wealth and the economic welfare of the country that invests, and of the rest of the world.[34]

Approximately a third of the book is devoted to the calculation of British foreign investments during the period 1870-1912,

[33] To determine this, Coats deducts from the value of exports the total amount payable by Canada for services; and from imports, all such income receivable by Canada. The net figures are then compared to find the amount by which the country fell short of meeting its international obligations year after year, and the aggregate deficit for the period as a whole. For excerpts from Coats' report, see Appendix A, pp. 154-156.

[34] Hobson, C. K., *Export of Capital,* January, 1914, pp. ix-xi. For excerpts from Hobson's summary tables, see Appendix A, pp. 156-157.

and to an explanation of the statistical methods used in this calculation. These figures are then used in a discussion of the relation between the capital exports and home industry of Great Britain. With the exception of a short introduction covering the broad purposes of the study, the rest of the book is given over to a discussion of the theoretical and historical aspects of the question.

V. Extending and Improving Scientific Methods

The compilation and presentation of the international accounts has been looked upon by some investigators as a problem in statistical method and as a means of furthering the scientific study of economic theory. In particular, this is true of the work done under the auspices of the International Statistical Institute, an "unofficial organization established with the general object of promoting the development of administrative and scientific statistics."

One of the founders of this organization, and for years its president, was Luigi Bodio, sometimes known as the "father of Italian statistics"; a man who was also founder of the national statistical office of Italy, and for many years Director General of Statistics in Italy. Bodio gave some attention to the question of the international accounts in the most important of his monographs on the indices of economic progress in Italy,[35] and, in common with other Italian economists and statisticians, took great interest in developing methods for estimating the items in the Italian accounts.

Another Italian member of the Institute who has done notable work in this field is Bonaldo Stringher, for some years a high official of the Italian treasury, and, since 1902, Director General of the Bank of Italy. Stringher was the author of the first complete study of the international accounts of Italy

[35] See 2d edition of *Di alcuni indici misuratori del movimento economico in Italia,* Rome, 1891, particularly chapters II and V.

to be made squarely for the purpose of testing as far as possible the adequacy of statistical data available in published and unpublished, official and unofficial sources. That is to say, his analysis was not incidental to any defense of tariff policy or related in any other way to the problem of the unfavorable trade balance. It was made in accordance with the effort being made by the leading statisticians in the Institute to arrive at a common method of constructing and testing the international accounts. The published results appear in the memorandum "Sur la balance des paiements entre l'Italie et l'étranger," presented at the meeting of the Institute held at The Hague in 1910.[36]

Perhaps the member of the Institute most widely known for his studies in this field was Alfred Neymarck, the eminent French statistician, who was particularly interested in the problem of estimating existing international debts and investments of various countries. At the meeting of the Institute in 1891, he called attention to the fact that, while a great deal was being done toward the collection of other statistics, no systematic effort was being made toward assembling information of this character. Four years later, at a meeting of the Institute, he presented a paper on the subject and also put through a motion that a committee be appointed to carry on this work. At every meeting thereafter until the outbreak of the war, the question was formally discussed by Neymarck and various of his associates, among whom should be mentioned Gruber, Bateman, Van de Borght, and Yves Guyot, as well as Bodio and Stringher. In all, he himself made ten reports to the Institute on this subject, the material which he presented

[36] *Bulletin de l'Institut international de Statistique,* Vol. XIX, Part 3, p. 93 ff. In somewhat more extended form, and with a long discussion of the significance of the unfavorable trade balance, Stringher's study appears in Vol. III of the collaborative study *Cinquanti anni di storia italiana,* Rome, 1911. For detailed discussion of the content of this report see McGuire, C. E., *Italy's International Economic Position,* pp. 265-271.

gradually cumulating so that the data in his paper for the meeting at Vienna in 1913 cover most of the countries of the world.[37]

At one of the meetings of the Institute, Dr. Ignaz Gruber, of Austria, raised the whole question of the purpose and content of the international accounts.[38] He presented a comprehensive report on the international balance of accounts of Austria-Hungary, and in this connection, called attention to the fact that, even among statisticians and economists particularly interested in the subject, there was no agreement as to the factors that such accounts should include, or the particular purpose they should be intended to serve. He suggested that their purpose might be defined as an attempt to determine the economic balance of nations. This suggestion led to a discussion of the meaning of the term "the economic balance of nations," and on a motion by Gruber, a committee was appointed to follow up this discussion. When the war broke out, however, no satisfactory solution had yet been reported back to the Institute.

The questions of the broader purposes, the content, and the form of the accounts had thus been raised in the discussions of the Institute and in independent studies of the question, but there was still considerable lack of agreement on many of these points.

[37] *Bulletin de l'Institut international de Statistique,* 1913, Vol. XX, Part II. As a rule he based his estimates upon security market data and government debt statements, but he supplemented these by available information of many different kinds.

[38] Tenth Session, held at London, in 1905.

CHAPTER III

PURPOSES SERVED SINCE 1913

During and since the war data have been compiled showing the debt and investment position and the income and outgo transactions of most of the nations of Europe and of many other countries as well. This chapter will cite some of the more important examples of the work done in the United States, Canada, and certain countries of Europe, and will show the purposes they were intended to serve.[1] The range of special problems thus covered has been extensive and varied, for during these 14 years the world has experienced practically all of the ills to which a pecuniarily organized society is subject. As a result, the need for more systematic studies of the accounts has been emphasized and recognized much more clearly than in the pre-war period.

I. Verifying Economic Theory

The primary purpose of one post-war group of studies has been the substantiation of the classical theory of international trade. All of these studies are the work of Harvard men, and all credit Professor F. W. Taussig with their inspiration.

In May, 1917, Dr. Taussig outlined a modification of the usual statement of the theory to adapt it to conditions prevailing under a régime of depreciated paper. Dr. John H. Williams, then a student at Harvard, had already begun a

[1] A complete bibliography of post-war studies dealing with the international accounts would comprise a list many times as extensive as the one covered by the citations in this chapter.

study of the Argentine "balance of payments" for the purpose of testing Professor Taussig's theory. He published this study, *Argentine International Trade Under Inconvertible Paper Money, 1880-1900*, in the spring of 1920, and in the meantime had published a complementary article on the balance of payments of certain Latin-American countries during the war.[2] In May, 1922, he reviewed the post-war foreign trade experience of Germany, the purpose again apparently being further to test the theory of foreign exchange under inconvertible paper.[3] In the preceding February, with the same general purpose in view, Dr. Frank D. Graham had published a study of the balance of payments of the United States covering the period of depreciated currency from 1862 to 1879.[4] The next in the series, and up to the present time the last one to appear, is Jacob Viner's book, *Canada's Balance of International Indebtedness in 1900-13*. In this, Dr. Viner undertakes an "inductive verification" of the "classical explanation of the mechanism of international trade" as it applies to trade between gold standard countries, "its treatment of Canadian matters (being) incidental to its main purpose."

II. Analyzing War and Reconstruction Problems

Most of the studies published since 1913 have been inspired by the exigencies of war, or by post-war problems of debts and reparations. During the war a great impetus was given to statistical work of all kinds, and particularly to that of the international accounts. People were extremely anxious over the enormous trade deficits of some of the countries and the way in which these deficits were being met. And in connection

[2] "Latin American Foreign Exchange and International Balances during the War," *Quarterly Journal of Economics*, May, 1919.

[3] "German Foreign Trade and the Reparation Payments," *Quarterly Journal of Economics*, May, 1922.

[4] *ibid.*, 1922, pp. 220-273. For excerpt from Graham's summary table see Appendix A, p. 158.

with post-war problems of debts and reparations, the everyday discussions of newspapers and magazines are giving considerable prominence to the international accounts of various countries.

The reparation question necessarily centered attention upon the international accounts of Germany. Even before the Armistice, however, the war needs of that country had already aroused interest in the subject. In the summer of 1916, for example, the government had seen the necessity of mobilizing under government control as many of the foreign investments of the German people as possible, and during the summer of 1916 had taken a census of the securities involved.[5] With the signing of the Armistice agreement, the remnant of German-owned foreign securities became of general interest in connection with the reparation discussions. As time passed, there were many who recognized that this remnant must be dwindling away through the use made of the securities in meeting the country's post-war requirements for foreign bills. But there were many who charged that, through the sale of paper marks and the revival of foreign trade, the country was accumulating foreign bills, foreign bank balances, and other investments abroad, in excess of the amount sacrificed. The trend of the argument was that although Germany was fully able to pay, she was wilfully evading the just claims of the Allies. To examine this charge, a knowledge of the war and post-war international accounts of the country was required.

It is well known that many such studies were made by the experts attached to the Reparation Commission,[6] but for the most part these were kept in unpublished form in the files of the Commission. A number of independent studies were published, however, of outstanding importance being those by

[5] This census was taken in accordance with a decree of August 23, 1916. See *Wirtschaft und Statistik,* No. 2, 1923, p. 64; and also Moulton and McGuire, *Germany's Capacity to Pay,* pp. 279 and 288.

[6] Professor Maurice Frère and others.

von Glasenapp,[7] formerly vice-president of the Reichsbank, J. M. Keynes,[8] and Kurt Singer,[9] all of which deal with the international financial position of Germany in the early months of 1922. A little later appeared the Institute of Economics study, *Germany's Capacity to Pay,* in which the international accounts of Germany from 1894 to 1922 are given for their bearing on the reparation problem. This was followed in the spring of 1924 by the report of the Second Committee of Experts, appointed by the Reparation Commission.[10] Like the preceding studies mentioned, this report was concerned with estimating the value of Germany's foreign investments (or rather, balances), and their relations to her capacity to pay. And in 1926 has appeared a study of Germany's international accounts for the year 1925, whose purpose is to show how Germany has been able to transfer abroad the sums required of her under the terms of the Dawes Plan, and to throw light upon the question of future payments.[11]

In the succession states, reparation requirements have raised much uneasy discussion of the international accounts. These states, which in large part have been carved out of the territory of Germany's former ally, the old Austro-Hungarian Monarchy, find that the war has left them weak and disorganized. Even the maintenance of an independent national existence within the boundaries fixed by the peace treaties has seemed for some of them a matter very difficult to achieve. This question in fact was made the subject of special inquiry in Austria, where, in 1925, Professor Friedrich Hertz of Vienna published an

[7] *Manchester Guardian Commercial, Reconstruction in Europe,* 1922, pp. 28-29.

[8] *ibid.,* p. 481.

[9] Die deutsche Auslands-Verschuldung. *Wirtschaftsdienst,* July 7, 1922, pp. 660-661.

[10] See Moulton, Harold G., *The Reparation Plan,* Appendix B, for a reprint of this report, and Chapter III for an analysis of its findings.

[11] Heichen, Dr. Arthur, *Deutschlands Zahlungsbilanz 1925.*

important essay entitled "Austria's Balance of Payments and her Capacity for Independent Existence." [12]

In Hungary studies by Dr. Alois Szaboky, Director of the Royal Hungarian Statistical Office, and Professor Friedrich von Fellner of the University of Budapest, have been used by the Hungarian Government in negotiating with the Reparation Commission concerning Hungary's capacity for meeting reparation payments, and the allocation of pre-war and war debts of the Austro-Hungarian Monarchy.[13]

For Rumania Professor I. N. Angelescu (Rector of the Academy of Commercial and Industrial Studies) has published an important study entitled "Rumania's Balance of Payments in Relation to Her Economic Policy." [14] The question at issue here is the relationship between Rumania's international accounts and the fluctuations in her currency.

In 1925 Dr. Karl Uhlig of Karlsbad made a study for Czechoslovakia, his primary purpose being to determine the extent to which foreigners—particularly Austrians—still held investments in Czechoslovak banks and industrial enterprises.[15] To this end, he made a careful analysis of the way in which the favorable trade balances for the five preceding years had been utilized.

In Italy the post-war accounts have been used as documentary evidence in debt funding negotiations. As discussions of Italy's debt to the United States and Great Britain progressed,

[12] Hertz, Friedrich, *Zahlungsbilanz und Lebensfähigkeit Oesterreichs*, Munich, 1925.

[13] See, for example, *Mémoire du Gouvernement Royal Hongrois concernant la répartition entre les États Successeurs de la dette publique de l'ancienne Hongrie*, 1922; also *Exposé addressé à la Commission des Réparations par le Ministre des Finances du Royaume, Hongrois, Tibor de Kallay*, 1923.

[14] In *Analele Statistice si Economice*, Bucharest, January-February, 1925.

[15] This study is entitled "Allgemeine Charakteristik der tschechoslowakischen Zahlungsbilanz," and was kindly placed at our disposal in manuscript form

frequent references were made by statesmen, financiers, and economists to the difficulties that would be involved in the transfers of payments. Thus interest in the post-war international accounts of the country began to take concrete form. The principal independent study growing out of these discussions was one by Giorgio Mortara, of the University of Rome, which was based on published data which proved to be unsatisfactory and incomplete.[16] During 1923-24 the government decided to have the whole subject thoroughly examined, the first result of this being a tabular digest made by Professor Pasquale Jannaccone of the University of Turin.[17] The memorandum upon which this tabular summary was based appears never to have been published, although the Minister of Finance announced it at the time as forthcoming. Other studies by Jannaccone were made for the use of the government during the course of 1924 and 1925, and these, as well as other investigations, formed the basis for a very comprehensive survey of Italy's international accounts, prepared by Professor Gino Borgatta at Pisa for the use of the Italian Government in the winter of 1925-26 in dealing with the World War Debt Funding Commission of the United States and with the Chancellor of the Exchequer of England.[18] Even more than was the case with the earlier studies of Director General Stringher, the memorandum of Professor Borgatta was based upon the fullest possible review of published and unpublished data which ordinarily would not be accessible to unofficial

[16] Published in the *Rivista Bancaria* of Milan, February 20, 1924. For a fuller discussion of this and other Italian studies mentioned, see McGuire, C. E., *Italy's International Economic Position*, 1926, particularly Appendices A and C.

[17] *Documenti sulla condizione finanziaria ed economica dell, 'Italia*, Rome, December, 1923, p. 10.

[18] This memorandum, which was printed in English at Rome, by the Ministry of Finance under the title *The Italian Balance of International Payments*, has had a very limited circulation, being intended almost exclusively for official use.

investigators—in particular, data on emigrants' remittances, banking transactions, shipping earnings, and official expenditures abroad.[19] Finally, a study was made by C. E. McGuire, of the Institute of Economics, in which the whole question of Italy's international accounts—for the pre-war, war, and post-war periods—was reviewed for its bearing upon the international economic position of the country.[20]

The Russian debt problem is responsible for one post-war study of the international accounts of Russia. In their book, *Russian Debts and Russian Reconstruction,* Leo Pasvolsky and Harold G. Moulton use Russia's pre-war international financial accounts as the basis for an evaluation of the probable Russian balance of payments when that country is restored to her pre-war level of production. In this manner they arrive at certain tentative conclusions as to Russia's probable capacity for making the necessary payments on her past and future foreign debts.

War and post-war fluctuations in French exchange have been particularly important in bringing attention to the accounts of France. Debt funding negotiations have further emphasized the need for information concerning the international financial affairs of the country. Available data for France have, therefore, been closely scrutinized.

Early in the war, M. René Pupin became interested in a statistical evaluation of the effects of the war on the country's national wealth, an interest which led him to estimate the pre-war international income and outgo of the country. Later on the instability of French exchange turned his attention to

[19] Of particular interest in connection with recent Italian investigation in this field are the various studies of the Ministry of Finance on holdings of foreign securities as reported in Tax Returns. These studies appear in the *Bollettino di statistica e di legislazione comparata,* for example in the volume for 1923-24, No. IV; and the computations of the very well informed director of research of the Credito Italiano, Avv. M. Mazzuchelli, under the title *Dati finanziari italiani,* Milan, 1923.

[20] *Italy's International Economic Position,* 1926.

the war-time accounts.[21] The fall of the franc was likewise responsible for M. Jules Décamps' very thorough study of the 1923 accounts of France. M. Décamps had previously examined many of the items in the war and post-war accounts in his larger discussion of the exchange question, *Les changes étrangers,* published in 1922.[22] These studies led both Décamps and Pupin to conclude that the outstanding foreign obligations of France on private account were enormous. These findings were unacceptable to some French economists, however.

In February, 1925, the war and post-war accounts of the country were once more reviewed, and in 1926 the data given were again brought down to date. The author of these two articles, M. Pierre Meynial, while centering attention upon the problem of the franc, was primarily concerned with refuting Décamps' conclusions. His own contention is that war and post-war trade and service deficits of France have been met with practically no foreign selling of francs or of domestic securities.[23] On the other hand, study of French

[21] *Journal* de la Société de Statistique de Paris, 1916, pp. 394-398; and *Richesse privée et finances francaises,* 1919, pp. 25-36. Also, *l'Information Financière,* Sept. 8, 1922.

[22] "La crise du franc." *Révenue de Paris,* March, 1924, pp. 202-222. Frequent references to M. Décamps' estimates are made in Appendix A of *The French Debt Problem* by Harold G. Moulton and Cleona Lewis. See particularly pp. 361 and 375.

[23] *Revue d'Économie Politique,* January-February, 1925, and March-April, 1926. In large part, M. Meynial's case rests upon his recalculation of the value of French imports for the years 1914-1920. Since the war several writers have indulged in the practice of recalculating trade data in order to show that the true situation of some particular country was not as bad as it appeared to be. In 1922 and 1923, for example, many of those who argued that Germany was wilfully evading the payment of the reparation debt, rested their case largely on a recalculation of the German trade figures. See *The Economic Review of the Foreign Press* of August 17, 1923, and November 16, 1923. Meynial's position is discussed by Moulton and Lewis in *The French Debt Problem,* pp. 381-393, to which he replied in the *Revue d'Économie Politique,* January-February, 1926, pp. 145-151.

holdings of foreign securities and of foreign holdings of French securities published by *l'Information* early in 1925, roughly confirms the view of Pupin and Décamps. Here the data presented were based largely on a survey of transactions in the principal security markets of France. Their view is also supported by the Institute of Economics publication entitled *The French Debt Problem*, a book in which the international accounts of France—pre-war, war, and post-war—are summarized for their bearing upon the economic position of the country.[24]

III. Furnishing Continuous and Comparable Official Data

Appreciating the need for continuous and authoritative studies of the accounts, a number of countries have begun to compile and publish them regularly in an official and semi-official way. In the United States this work was initiated by the Harvard Committee on Economic Research, and was taken over by the government after four studies had already been issued.[25] In Great Britain the task has been handled in a semi-official way by the *Board of Trade Journal*.[26] And within the few years, a number of other governments have begun publishing the international accounts for their several countries.

[24] Moulton and Lewis, *The French Debt Problem*, 1925.

[25] See studies published in the *Review of Economic Statistics*, Vols. I, II, III, IV, and V, and also Department of Commerce *Trade Information Bulletins*, Nos. 144, 215, 340, and 399. (See discussion in Appendix B.) An excellent unofficial study of the foreign investments of the United States is one entitled *American Foreign Investments*, by Robert W. Dunn.

[26] The first of these was published January 15, 1920. Unofficial studies of the war and post-war accounts of Great Britain that should be mentioned are one by John A. Hobson in the *Journal of Political Economy*, August, 1922, and three by Edgar Crammond, as follows: *The British Shipping Industry*, 1917; *Cantor Lectures*, 1918; and one published in the *Quarterly Review*, July, 1918, p. 190.

There are still a great many countries, however, where this work has not yet been taken up by the government but is being carried on by private initiative, or left undone.[27]

Much that has recently been accomplished toward the inclusion of this work within the field of government statistics is directly attributable to the efforts of the Economic and Financial Section of the League of Nations. This organization is now urging upon the governments of all countries the importance of compiling and publishing these accounts, and is attempting to co-ordinate and standardize the work. In the task that this group is undertaking, it recognizes a three-fold purpose: (1) to encourage as many countries as possible to furnish a statement of their accounts; (2) to improve and eventually standardize the methods employed for securing the data, and the form for presenting them; (3) to make these reports easily available in published form.[28]

Another semi-official group which has recently begun to take an active interest in the subject of the international accounts is the International Chamber of Commerce. About a year ago, the Committee on International Settlements of the International Chamber began a study of the international accounts of a group of countries with a view to ascertaining any discernible relations existing between inter-governmental debt payments and changes in other items in the international income account of the several debtor and creditor countries. After some preliminary investigation, it was decided

[27] For example, specific mention should be made here of the very excellent work being done by the banking firm of Ernesto Tornquist and Co., Ltd., in the compilation and presentation of the accounts of Argentina. This bank has for many years been indefatigable in its researches in this field.

[28] Memoranda were published by the League in 1924 covering the years 1910-1923; in 1925, covering 1910-1924; and in 1926, covering 1911-1925. The first of these included data—some official and some unofficial—for countries; the second, for nineteen countries; and the third, for twenty-two.

by the Committee that steps should be taken to obtain more nearly comparable data than now were available. At the Rome meeting, in 1923, the suggestion was made that if progress in this direction were to be made it would be necessary to have an international committee of economists. This suggestion was at once acted upon, the committee appointed being as follows: Henry A. E. Chandler of the United States, Dr. H. Bucher of Germany, John Maynard Keynes of Great Britain, Professor Charles Rist of France, and Professor Fernand Baudhuin of Belgium. The Italian member has not yet (April, 1927) been appointed.

The efforts now being made toward securing continuous and comparable data with regard to the international trade and financial transactions of various countries represent the outstanding development in this field during the war and post-war period. In contrast with what is thus promised for the future, a review of the work done in the past shows this to have been, on the whole, discontinuous and disconnected. For few countries, indeed, have accounts been published covering a consecutive period of as much as, say, ten, fifteen, or twenty-five years. And not only do the earlier studies, with some few exceptions, cover short and isolated periods of time; they also show considerable lack of uniformity in their form and content. As a rule, therefore, they cannot be easily pieced together into connected stories for the countries concerned.

One very effective reason for the lack of continuity in existing data for various countries is the fact that the work of compiling and presenting the international accounts of a country is an enormous one. It not only requires much time, energy, and initiative on the part of the investigator but, if satisfactory results are to be attained, it is also practically necessary that he have the co-operation of the many banks and business houses that are directly in touch with the situation. Such co-operation, for example, is needed in the compilation of

the basic data to be used in estimating the interest item in the accounts. But to secure such co-operation and to get adequate information on this one item alone, and for a single year, is a heavy task for one person to undertake. To bring this information down to date year after year would require a fair share of a man's working life. The interest item, however, is only one of the many items in the accounts. The investigator who would attempt to include all of the items in his statement of the accounts, and to draw up such a statement year after year, would indeed have undertaken a full-time job. Even government agencies have found their vast resources taxed by the difficulties of the work, and until recently have been content to make these studies only as special occasions required.

CHAPTER IV

FORM AND CONTENT DETERMINED BY PURPOSE

Before agreement can be reached concerning the data to be presented in the international accounts and their form of presentation, there must be agreement concerning the purposes they are to serve. This problem, as we have seen, did not face the pioneers in this field of economics and statistics. Their studies were made, for the most part, as special occasions demanded. Starting as they did with some particular question in mind, they saw the purposes of their work clearly defined at the beginning and shaped their investigations and reports of results to agree with this purpose.

Different investigators, however, had different problems to consider. One was interested in explaining an impending currency crisis, another in forecasting the probable outcome of some proposed currency or taxation measure, while another centered his attention upon helping solve some other problem of immediate interest. From these differences in purpose there were, as a matter of course, resulting differences both in the kind of data considered, and in the methods used in presenting these data. Thus some investigators confined their attention to studies of the international trade and service transactions of particular countries. Others were concerned primarily with ascertaining the foreign debt and investment position of the countries they were studying.[1] The outcome was that studies made for one purpose would have proved inadequate if they had been called into use in various other connections.

[1] For sample statements illustrating this point see Appendix A.

It is only within recent years that efforts have been made to arrive at an inclusive definition of the content and purpose of the accounts. Shortly before the war the International Institute of Statistics discussed at some length the desirability of arriving at an agreement on these points. Apparently, however, these discussions brought no tangible results. At present there is still great lack of uniformity in the accounts published by various agencies. And, as we have seen, the need for a standardized method of compiling and presenting the data is again up for consideration—both by the International Chamber of Commerce and by the League of Nations.[2] The question is a timely one, for now that government agencies are beginning the regular compilation and publication of the accounts, they must inquire whether or not the data can be compiled and presented in such a way that they will fairly well answer all the purposes for which they may be required. Obviously, a guide to the content and form of the account lies in an analysis of their purpose. In fact, agreement concerning the general purposes which the accounts are intended to serve is prerequisite to agreement concerning the items which they should include and the form in which they should be presented.

The main purposes served by the accounts may be grouped into three broad classes. This conclusion is based upon a review of the various investigations cited in Chapters II and III and also upon a survey of current opinion concerning the value of the work and the need that exists for more thorough and extensive studies of the accounts of certain countries.

1. The accounts are needed by the government and people of a country as an aid in explaining certain developments in the country's economic life and in analyzing the probable effects of proposed measures. Practically all of the investigations cited in Chapter II, and a number of those referred to in Chapter III, were made for this general purpose. For example, in

[2] Discussed at some length on pp. 41-42.

some cases, as we have seen, the purpose was to furnish explanation of some impending currency crisis and to find what might be done to right the situation. Others were made to show the probable outcome of some proposed currency reform, such, for example, as the adoption of the gold standard, the resumption of specie payments, or some similar step. Some were made to analyze the effects of a country's foreign trade and service operations upon its foreign investments. And for still others the purpose was to forecast the results of some suggested tax measure.

Post-war developments emphasize the fact that financiers, economists, and statesmen find in the international accounts one of the several indexes needed for explaining current economic developments and for outlining future policies which they would have their respective countries follow. Not only has the number of published investigations increased enormously since the war, but also there is an increasing tendency for writers discussing questions of the internal policy of a country to utilize existing studies of the international trade and financial relations of the country before arriving at conclusions.

So far as Great Britain is concerned, the importance of the accounts is frequently referred to in no uncertain terms. Since the war that country has been striving to stabilize the pound at par, to retain her position in the trade and financial markets of the world, and, in short, to bring the country to a level of general prosperity at least equal to that of the pre-war period. Not long ago, the *Monthly Review* of the Midland Bank Limited, in discussing the means by which the successful stabilization of the currency had been effected, emphasized the importance of the international accounts in the explanation of this phenomenon. "All sorts of theories, fantastic and scientific, have been put forward to explain the continued steadiness of the pound. . . . The guide to a solution of the problem is provided by estimates of overseas demand for

sterling and British requirements of external currencies—in a word, the balance of international payments." [3]

The City Editor of the *Manchester Guardian Commercial* commented with equal assurance upon the usefulness of the accounts for their bearing upon the question of the general standard of living of the country. He said:

> At the present time this question of the "balance of payments" is of even greater practical import than usual, since, if it is true that the balance is against us, then we must be meeting it by borrowing abroad or, which comes to much the same thing, disposing of part of our accumulated foreign investments; and if we are doing that we are obviously approaching the time when we shall be driven to curtail our imports and to content ourselves with a lower general standard of living. The only approach to a positive solution of the problem is that provided by a calculation made by the Board of Trade each year of the various invisible items entering into the foreign trade account—earnings of British shipping, net income from overseas investments, banking commissions, and so on.[4]

In Germany, since the war, the government has taken a very active part in discouraging the flotation of foreign loans by German municipalities. This policy is dictated in large measure by studies of the international accounts which show that the international income of the country for years to come will, in all probability, be entirely absorbed by existing obligations; in such circumstances, new loans would necessarily mean future embarrassment. In Italy, the need for increasing the available supply of foreign exchange has been in part responsible for the government's policy of encouraging the emigration of some of its people. Not only is it intended thus to ease the pressure of population at home, but it is also hoped that the supply of foreign bills will be increased through resulting increases in the amount of funds sent home by emigrant Italians.

[3] *Monthly Review* of the Midland Bank Limited, October-November, 1926.

[4] *Manchester Guardian Commercial,* November 4, 1926, p. 542.

In the United States, interest in the international accounts has largely centered around the loans being granted to foreigners, their present and future significance to the country, and policies that should be adopted regarding them. One writer, in commending the State Department for requesting bankers to furnish prompt information concerning prospective foreign loans, points out the importance of complete information of this sort.

> These loans have two aspects, on the one hand the dollars which are thereby made available to foreigners to buy our goods and to pay their debts here, and on the other hand the foreign securities which are received by American investors in exchange for their dollars. . . . As these investments grow, in the aggregate, into many billions of dollars, a situation is created which cannot but influence our foreign policy. No foreign policy could be intelligently conceived and carried out by a Department of State which was ignorant of or indifferent to the past and current acquisitions by Americans of interest in foreign lands. It might well be that such a movement with respect to some particular country might attain proportions such that it would tend to deprive our Government of its freedom of action in dealing with certain foreign problems and in carrying out some foreign policy which, from other aspects, would be of major national importance. The Department of State should have such information as would enable it to protect against such a development.[5]

Information of the sort collected by the State Department is, of course, only a part of that which is usually thought of as coming under the head of the International Accounts. On the other hand, the Department of Commerce has undertaken to summarize and publish data concerning all loans actually floated, as well as data concerning foreign investments in the securities and enterprises of this country and concerning the international trade and service transactions of the country.

[5] Dulles, John Foster, "Our Foreign Loan Policy," *Foreign Affairs*, October, 1926.

These data are given wide publicity by the newspapers here and abroad, and are much discussed generally for their bearing upon questions of production, prices, and general well-being. They are looked upon as a part of the necessary and useful information required by bankers and business men who are debating what their own future line of action shall be with regard to foreign loans and foreign trade.

2. The international accounts may sometimes be required as evidence of the credit standing of a country negotiating a foreign loan. They furnish the prospective lender with part of the data required for forming an opinion regarding the credit risks that would be involved in granting the desired loan. This use is still quite new. No case is cited in preceding chapters of an investigation made specifically for this purpose. It may be added, however, that the idea of a systematic credit analysis as a necessary antecedent to the extension of a loan is a development of comparatively recent date even in the field of business.

The international accounts alone will not, of course, supply all of the information which the lenders should have as a basis for a credit analysis of this sort. Capacity to pay foreign obligations is a two-part problem. Internal affairs determine the availability of funds within the country. The international situation of the country determines the ease or difficulty with which the transfer problem will be met: the problem of converting these domestic funds into a form that will be acceptable by the foreign creditor. These, of course,are almost axiomatic statements that are now becoming generally familiar through post-war discussions of debts and reparation payments.

As was pointed out in Chapter I, there is only one form in which, as a long-run proposition, the transfer of payment can be made across the frontier of a country—in the form of goods and services. For a limited time real payment can be made through the sacrifice of the "international assets," or foreign investments of the country, but this involves a decrease in the

country's interest income, and, therefore, in its future capacity to pay. Information concerning ability to transfer payments by either or both of these methods should be readily available from the international financial statements of the country.

A good illustration of the fact that the international accounts are, at the present time, actually being used for this purpose may be found in the recent discussion of a proposed plan for marketing the German railway bonds provided for under the Dawes Plan, and for using the proceeds in settling the whole debt and reparation problem. A cablegram from Berlin dated September 25, 1926, to the *New York Times* says:

> The official Trade Conditions Institute last week published statistics showing that the foreign-payment balance of Germany between the date of stabilization in 1923 and the end of June, 1926, was adverse to Germany by the large total of 5,585,000,000 marks. This deficit had to be met by contracting abroad 2,544,000,000 marks of long-term loans, by recalling 1,200,000,000 marks of capital hoarded abroad, and by other capital transactions of 1,625,000,000 marks, including investments of foreign capital directly in Germany.
>
> On the basis of these figures the financial press seems to agree that no mobilization of the Dawes bonds would be possible unless the United States were to take the leadership in arranging it. As to the probability of that, the comment of financial circles is that Wall Street, in view of the large interest payments already contracted for the account of German industrial bonds placed in the American market, might raise the objection that mobilization of the railway bonds would threaten Germany's ability to keep on paying interest on its already outstanding obligations.

Decision upon the proposed new foreign loan to Germany apparently will be made in accordance with the results shown by an analysis of the international credit position of the country, and a most important factor in this analysis is the situation shown by the international accounts.

In time the international accounts of a country as a whole

may, and should, come to be regarded as part of the necessary credit information to be taken into consideration in passing upon the credit standing of some political division of the country, or some one of its corporations, seeking to borrow in a foreign market. If the country as a whole has a deficiency of exports—including both commodities and services—this deficiency will have to be met by borrowing abroad. And if these borrowings cannot be funded on a satisfactory basis, depreciation of the currency will inevitably follow. This, unless it is soon checked, will have its effects upon the foreign paying capacity of all within the country. The following case will illustrate this point.

In 1923, the State of Santa Catharina, Brazil, successfully negotiated a loan in the United States. The foreign debt history of the state was good. Its assets and resources seemed sufficient to warrant the assumption of this new liability, and along with this was the fact that the state had always been regarded as a good risk. The credit analysis made, however, gave too little weight to the fact that Brazil as a nation has a large foreign debt; that she must have a large excess of commodity exports to meet payments on this debt; and that one of her most important exports, coffee, is subject to wide price fluctuations. As goes coffee, so goes the milreis. Some time after the granting of the loan, coffee fell in price and Brazilian exchange dropped.[6] The milreis taxes collected by the State of Sta. Catharina were insufficient to meet the budgetary needs of the state and provide payment on her foreign loans. Interest payments on the new loan were suspended, and have thus far not been resumed—though resumption in the near future is expected. Had these facts been taken account of in the preliminary analysis, it is still possible that the loan might have been granted—but in that case the stoppage of interest would not have come as an unexpected event.

[6] The revolution in southern Brazil probably exaggerated this situation —but did not bring it about.

3. The international accounts are used in times of stress to show the extent to which existing foreign obligations can be met. A number of studies made for this purpose are cited in Chapter III. In particular, as is shown there, the accounts of Germany have been scrutinized again and again to determine the maximum reparation payments that might be exacted without bringing about a total collapse of the German economic system. And the Dawes report, which clearly stipulates that the payments required must be kept within Germany's capacity to pay, specifically refers to the importance of the international accounts in determining the volume of payments that may be transferred to foreign countries at any given time.

This use of the accounts has been particularly in the foreground in post-war international-debt negotiations. The World War Foreign Debt Commission, in arranging settlements with a number of the countries debtor to the United States, has proceeded upon the assumption that the schedule of payments to be drawn up should be based upon the paying capacity of the countries concerned. In line with this position, the Italian Debt Funding Mission to the United States presented voluminous documents on the subject of Italy's limited capacity to pay. The resources of the country were discussed to show what strict limitations these set upon the amounts that might be collected within the country. Her international accounts were presented to show the narrow margin available for effecting a transfer to foreigners of the sums to be collected. Likewise, the French Debt Funding Mission under M. Bérenger brought with them a document entitled *France and Her Capacity to Pay*, approximately one-fourth of which is devoted to the international accounts of France in 1913, 1923, and 1924, and the probable state of the accounts in the future.

The accounts regularly published by governmental agencies should be designed to serve all of these three types of uses. If this can be accomplished, the annual data published for a given country should prove roughly comparable over a series

of years, and there is also hope that eventually valid comparisons may be made of the accounts published for different countries. With the statisticians of all countries working consistently to make their studies meet this inclusive definition of purpose, it is unlikely that important data will be omitted by any of them. And furthermore, common acceptance of a definition broad enough to cover all specific uses or purposes, should in time make international co-operation in the compilation and checking of the data a feasible undertaking.

It may at first glance seem that two groups of studies referred to in Chapters II and III have been overlooked in the present discussion. No mention has been made of the pre-war methodological studies published by members of the International Institute of Statistics, nor of the group of theoretical studies that have appeared since the war. These, however, can scarcely be said to represent independent uses which need to be considered. The question of methodology must, of course, always be kept in mind, but only because better data and better methods of presenting these data are needed for other purposes. And obviously, if the published accounts for various countries are adequate for the analysis of current economic problems and as an aid in forecasting future economic developments, and if they furnish basic information required for a credit analysis or for an analysis of capacity to meet existing obligations, they will also serve the theoretical economists—for it is with the theoretical implications of problems such as these that he is concerned.

For deciding upon the form and content of the international accounts, a useful analogy is found in corporation finance. Like the international accounts, the system of accounts devised for an ordinary business corporation must serve a variety of purposes. The shareholders and officers of a corporation expect and demand periodic reports showing the financial position of the business at the end of each accounting period, and in comparison with that of the preceding period. Such a set of reports

presents in summary form the information that is given in more detail in the books of the corporation. A complete set of such reports is usually referred to as the "financial statement." A complete set of reports setting forth the international accounts for a period may likewise be referred to as the "international financial statement" for a given country.

From the point of view of management, the purposes served by the financial statement of a corporation are very much like those for which the international financial statement of a country is required.

1. It helps point out what is happening in the business, and thus puts the management in a position to exercise a definite and sure control over its own affairs. Under this broad head may be grouped all the various problems that concern the present and future internal policy of the concern. And, as in the case of the international financial statement, this is the use most commonly made of the statement, and the one for which it is regularly required.

2. A corporation desiring to borrow money at a bank or to float a loan in the securities markets must furnish the banker with data from which he can form an opinion regarding the credit risk that would be involved in granting the desired loan.

3. A debtor corporation that cannot meet its obligations when pressed by its creditors, must furnish a financial statement on the basis of which the creditors will decide what line of action they will adopt. All in all, they furnish an index of the financial standing of the corporation at a given time; just as the international financial statement furnishes one of the indexes upon which the international financial standing of a given country can be judged.

So far as the corporation is concerned, it is generally agreed that if its reports are to meet these purposes, they must set forth certain clearly defined types of information. They must show the net worth of the corporation—the net value of assets over and above offsetting claims by outsiders. They must show

the amount by which this net figure has increased or decreased as a result of financial operations during the given period. They must explain how these changes have been brought about. That is, they should show what operations have been productive of income, what the various classes of expenditures have been, and how income and expenditures for the period compare with those for the preceding period. They should also show the form that new assets or new liabilities have taken; whether net earnings have been invested in real estate, in machinery and equipment, in securities, or are in the form of cash in hand or in the bank; and whether the several classes of debts have been reduced or increased.

The presentation of the corporation financial statement has been the subject of much discussion. With regard to the larger points of method, there is general agreement, although there are differences of opinion on certain issues. The question now is whether conclusions concerning the content and presentation of the international financial statement cannot be based upon current practice in corporation accounting.

CHAPTER V

FORM AND CONTENT OF THE FINANCIAL STATEMENT

What should be the content of the international financial statement, and how should it be presented in order that it may best meet its purpose? This is the question raised for discussion in Chapter V. Continuing the comparison made in Chapter IV, the analysis which follows is made in terms of standardized usage in the field of business accounting. An objection may, of course, be raised to this procedure. Some may hold that recent studies of the "balance of payments" and "balance of accounts" of different countries have already made as full use of accounting forms and terminology as is practicable, and that nothing will be gained by exploring the subject further. So far as superficial details are concerned this objection would no doubt hold good. But with regard to the essentials of the financial statement, judgment must be suspended until these essentials have been discussed. In Chapter VI some recent balance of payments statements may then be examined from the point of view of their content and form, and in comparison with the financial statement used in the field of business.

I. The Two Essentials of a Financial Statement

The financial statement which practically every business prepares at regular intervals for the use of its owners and executives is made up of two separate reports: the balance sheet and the income statement. The balance sheet lists the

value of the assets and liabilities at a particular time, the difference between these representing the *net worth* of the business—thus it shows the financial condition of the concern at a given moment. The income statement itemizes the sources of income and expenditure over a period of time, the excess of income over expenditure, or vice versa, indicating the *change* that has taken place in net assets or liabilities.

A comparison of two balance sheets, one for the beginning and one for the end of a certain period will, of course, measure the increase or decrease in the net worth of the business during that time. It also shows the extent to which the change is reflected in the several classes of assets and liabilities. But the explanation of these changes is set forth in the income statement.[1]

These two reports constitute the two essential parts of the financial statement that has been devised by the accountant and adopted by business. Either one taken alone is incomplete. Together they serve the purposes (discussed in Chapter IV) for which the financial statement is required. The question is whether a complete financial statement of this sort is required in international finance.

In its international relations a country—including both its government and its people—carries on a vast number and variety of transactions with other countries.[2] As we have seen,

[1] In practice it is sometimes very difficult to distinguish between capital expenditures and outlays which should be charged to operating expense.

[2] The word "transaction" is used here and elsewhere in this book in its accounting sense. "We may define transaction as an exchange of values. It may be between persons, as when a sale is made, or it may be between accounts within the business itself. . . . Some authors further analyze transactions as *completed* when the bargain is fully consummated between the parties, as when delivery is made and the money is paid in cash; or *incomplete,* as where something still remains to be done by either or both parties to the transaction. In this latter case, claims or rights of action arise to protect the parties until full consummation is made. But, since from the accounting standpoint a claim or right

it buys and sells commodities and services. It makes extensions of credit in various forms, and makes investments in foreign securities and foreign enterprises. And vice versa, it borrows from foreigners in various ways and foreigners invest their funds in its securities and its enterprises. Looked at in this way it has many of the attributes of a business enterprise, and for our purpose may be thought of as a gigantic trading concern. Its assets are the claims it holds against foreign countries, whether in the form of long or short-time loans of various classes, or direct investment in foreign enterprises. Its liabilities are the claims which foreign governments and foreign people hold against its government and people.

The people of this country, as we have seen in preceding chapters, will frequently have need for data showing how these assets and liabilities compare—and the total of each—thus it would seem that they will have need for a balance sheet. They will also require information concerning the results of current trade and service transactions, but this is the information that would be furnished by an international income account.

A. The Balance Sheet, or Statement of Foreign Debts and Investments

There is nothing particularly new in the idea of using the international debt and investment statement of a nation to throw light upon its international financial position at a given time. Various investigators have done this, as we have seen in Chapter II. But on the whole, few investigators have seen the advantage to be gained from treating this debt and investment statement as the international "balance sheet" of the country.[3]

is one kind of property or asset, there is little need of this finer analysis." Kester, R. B., *Accounting Theory and Practice*, Vol. I, pp. 63-64.

[3] The balance sheet for the country as a whole (corresponding to the consolidated balance sheet of an industrial corporation and its subsidiary trading corporation) would include not only the *international* assets, but *all* assets of every sort, or the total national wealth of the

In international finance, as a matter of fact, the term "international balance sheet" has often been loosely applied to a statement containing income and outgo items. This confusion of terminology probably resulted from the fact that in the early days attention had been fixed upon the "balance of trade." When the importance of other items of income and outgo began to be recognized, this narrower term was replaced by the broader one of "balance of payments" or "balance of accounts." In their strict sense, these terms were meant to characterize only one item, the balancing item, in the account. In practice, however, they became pretty generally used as titles for the whole statement.

"Balance of payments" was often shortened to "balance sheet," but as a rule the account in question was neither an income statement nor a balance sheet. Items representing all varieties and kinds of international transactions might be jumbled into it all together. Into a single so-called balance sheet, in short, were stowed away items representing all of the various classes of international income and outgo, along with items representing increases and decreases in international liabilities and increases and decreases in international assets.[4]

This mixed account proved to be very misleading. It gave less information about the trend of affairs than can be extracted from the ordinary *trial balance* which the accountant takes off the ledger as a preliminary step towards making up the income statement and balance sheet. But it was interpreted by many

country. The other side of the account would be made up of (1) the international liabilities, and (2) the "net worth" of the country, or net national wealth after allowance had been made for all foreign claims. For example, Giffen's study of the international accounts in 1878 (see pp. 22-23) was incidental to his study of the total national wealth of Great Britain, and Helfferich's study of 1913 (see pp. 25-26) was incidental to his study of the national wealth of Germany.

[4] For a "balance sheet" illustrating this point, see Appendix A, p. 158.

readers— and no doubt, in many cases, by its authors as well— as if it had been a complete financial statement.[5] The trouble was, of course, that good accounting principles were not being followed. The writers were trying to get along with a single account, despite the fact that they wished to present data which would have been much more easily understood and interpreted if set forth in two separate accounts.

The term "balance sheet," as it is used in international finance, should agree with good usage in the general field of accounting. Looked at from this point of view, the balance sheet should include both international assets and international liabilities; and no classes of assets or liabilities should be omitted. And, as a matter of course, none of the explanatory items—or what the bookkeeper calls "profit and loss" items—should be included.

This, we may say, is a standard that has very seldom been achieved in the debt and investment studies published in the past. And anticipating what is to follow in Chapter VI, we may also say that none of the agencies now regularly publishing the international accounts for various countries has thus far seen fit to include in these accounts a complete balance sheet of this sort. On the whole it has been customary for the debt and investment studies to take account of only some one large class of balance sheet items, to the exclusion of all others. Such studies for Italy, for example, and for pre-war United States, were in the main confined to liability items of a long-time character. For France, Germany, and Great Britain, long-term foreign loans and investments were all that were likely to be included.[6] To take a concrete case—already referred to in Chapter II—the very detailed study made in 1902 by the French Ministry of Foreign Affairs, gives data for what

[5] Perhaps a better comparison may be made between this account and the classified summary taken from the bookkeeper's "journal."

[6] For excerpt from a study illustrating this point see Appendix A, pp. 142-143.

the corporation accountant would call the "fixed assets"; but omits short-term loans of all kinds, and all liability items.

With all classes of international debts and investments included, the international balance sheet, of course, gives a complete picture of the international financial standing of a country at a given time.[7] This, as a matter of fact, was exactly the information that was really required for answering some of the questions that gave rise to a number of the earlier debt and investment studies. In discussions of the currency question, for example, it was of greater importance to know the *net* amount of a country's foreign assets or liabilities, than it was to know the *total* of either one alone. For certain purposes, however, it is not sufficient to know the state of affairs at a given moment, it is necessary also to know something of the trend of affairs.

To be of maximum value, the international balance sheet should be compiled periodically. Are investments increasing or decreasing? Are obligations to foreigners being incurred or paid off? These are questions that arise in connection with many larger problems. A single balance sheet will not answer them, but they may be quickly disposed of by comparison of a number of balance sheets drawn up at regular intervals.

Neymarck's studies, to which reference has been made in Chapter II, more nearly meet this requirement than those made by any other investigator. His data are not presented in balance-sheet form, and in fact do not include all of the items that would be required for a complete balance sheet. Long-term obligations and investments are both included; short-term items are omitted—an omission probably due to the enormous difficulties involved in the collection of the data, rather than to a lack of appreciation of their value in connection with his inquiries. But the important point is that Neymarck's studies, particularly those for France, give these balance-sheet data for a series of years. Thus they not only

[7] For a sample balance sheet see Chapter VII, p. 96.

show the state of affairs at some particular time, but they also indicate the rate of increase in the net foreign investments of the French people.

B. The International Income Account

In the field of accounting the income account is an elementary and fundamental concept. In international finance, however, the use of the term—with its various synonyms—is relatively new and apparently has not yet been fully accepted and adopted. Quite obviously, however, the idea that it represents was understood and made use of by many writers whose studies have already been referred to in Chapter II. Giffen's investigations, for example, were concerned almost entirely with the international income and outgo of Great Britain, and the accounts that he presents are income accounts in the strict sense of the term. No asset or liability items are to be found in them. But Giffen did not specifically call attention to this fact, and some of those who have followed him have fallen into errors that he avoided.

The international income account should be clearly distinguished from the international balance sheet. In corporation accounting as we have said, the income account is used to explain the changes that have taken places in the "net worth" of a business during a given period.[8] It summarizes and presents in classified form, all items of expenditure and all receipts of income, and shows the excess of the one over the other. The income account for a merchandising concern, for example, shows an inventory of goods on hand at the beginning of the period, cost of goods bought during the period, selling costs of all kinds and descriptions, including overhead costs of management, etc., and upkeep and depreciation on plant and equipment of all kinds. These are the expenditures items.

[8] The net worth of a business concern is defined as the excess of its assets over its liabilities.

The offsetting income items are receipts from sales during the period and the closing inventory showing value of goods on hand at the end of the period. The difference between the two sides of the account shows the net gain or loss from operations. It must, of course, exactly equal the change in net worth that is shown by a comparison of the balance sheets for the beginning and end of the period (aside from such adjustments as may be necessitated by dividends, stock sales, writing off and writing up of capital assets, and similar changes which are independent of the operating results). The income account is thus a report complementary to the balance sheet; but of the two reports that make up a complete financial statement it is in many cases the more important one.

The international income account, in agreement with good accounting practice, should, of course, present in summary form the items of international income and outgo of a country during a given period. In the main these items cover the trade and service transactions of a country.[9] They include imports and exports of commodities, imports and exports of gold and silver, interest on foreign debts and foreign investments, income and outgo for shipping services, for the tourist trade, and for banking and commission charges, immigrants' remittances and funds brought in by immigrants, remittances received from emigrants, funds brought into a country or taken away by migratory workers, gifts for charitable and relief purposes, reparation payments in money or in kind, and so on.[10] Thus compiled

[9] For a sample income account see Chapter VII, p. 94.

[10] Objection has been made by some writers to the inclusion of the "gifts" and the "reparation deliveries in kind" items. The reason given for this objection is that "neither gifts nor reparation deliveries in kind involve a debt or constitute a money claim." To answer this objection we must look at other items in the account. (1) If the gifts are made in the form of goods or gold, the foreign trade statistics of both the sending and receiving countries will record the movement of the commodities involved. Therefore, unless the "gifts" item is set down in the account the export statistics for the sending country will over-state

the account would show the extent to which current operations had provided funds for new investments abroad; or the extent to which they had necessitated the sacrifice of existing foreign investments or the contraction of new obligations to foreigners. It would thus show the net change that had been effected in the international debt or investment position of the country during the given period and would correspond, in its net amount, with the net change shown in a comparison of international balance sheets for the beginning and end of the period.

No such clear-cut story is told by the mixed account (referred to on page 59) so often presented under the head of a balance of payments, or balance of accounts, statement. For example, if such an account includes purchases and sales of securities along with items of income and outgo, then its balancing item will show the net increase or decrease in all other

the payments for exports that are due from other countries. On the other hand, the import statistics of the receiving country will over-state the amount that the country will have to pay out on account of imports. The same argument applies to the item "reparation deliveries in kind." If the commodities that are used in the direct payment of reparations are included in the trade figures of the countries concerned, the offsetting item "reparation deliveries in kind" must also be included in the account. Otherwise the unadjusted trade figures do not give a true statement of the situation. (2) If gifts are made in the form of paper money or securities, the international liabilities or debts of the sending country are correspondingly increased, while, on the other hand, the claims held by the receiving country are likewise increased. Unless an entry is made in the income account under some appropriate heading such as gifts, this account will carry no explanation for the change that has been made in the debts and investments items in the balance sheet. In other words, the income account and the comparative balance sheets for the period will fail to agree. (3) If gifts are made in the form of commodities carried by parcel post (see discussion on p. 112) they may entirely escape record in the trade statistics, and at the same time they make no change in the international assets and liabilities items for the countries concerned. In this case, of course, no entry should be made under the heading of gifts unless it is offset by a corresponding adjustment in the trade figures or the debt and investment estimates.

international assets or liabilities during the year. If this is the purpose of the account, well and good. As a rule, however, neither the investigator nor his readers has any particular interest in knowing what shift there has been in a limited group of international assets and liabilities. It is the net change in all classes of obligations and investments that is of importance for most purposes, and therefore it is an income account, strictly defined, that is needed.[11]

A question may be raised here concerning the handling of unusual losses of foreign investments—such, for example, as those suffered by a number of European countries during the world war—whether such losses should be carried through the income account, or whether the deduction should be shown on the balance sheet itself. This question, however, is of minor importance in connection with the international accounts.[12] The second method is probably preferable, and may be argued on the basis of legal decisions and accounting practice; although some argument may be advanced for the first method also. The point will be taken up again, however, in the more detailed discussion of Chapter VII.

C. Either Account Alone Is Incomplete

In the field of business the balance sheet is of particular interest to the creditor for it shows in detail the security that is back of his loan. But he also has need for the income account, showing and explaining the net profit earned or net losses incurred; for a losing concern is not likely to be a good credit risk. On the other hand, proprietors and stockholders

[11] On p. 57 we have already referred to the fact that in corporation accounting there are border-line cases where it is difficult to distinguish between capital expenditures and outlays which should be charged to operating expense.

[12] See Hatfield, Henry Rand, *Accounting*, 1927, Chapters X-XII, for a full discussion from the point of view of corporation accounting. Also see Chapter VII of this book, pp. 107-108.

are primarily interested in the income statement. But they have need also for a comparative balance sheet, showing the way in which earnings have affected assets and liabilities. A good showing in the income statement may have been produced at the expense of security, more desirable assets, for example, having been replaced by those of a less desirable kind. For the purposes of creditor and proprietor alike, therefore, either account is incomplete without the other.

The same is true in international finance. Neither account alone will serve the purposes for which the international financial statement is required. For example, the income account for a country with large investments abroad might show that income from this source was more than offset by net outgo for commodities and for other services. The income account would thus be of service both to the people and government of this country, and to their creditors. With the balance sheet showing that the country had long since passed to the stage of an investing country, the net deficit in the income account would serve as a warning of probable currency and exchange difficulties ahead. To take a second example, the income account of a country might show a large surplus; but its balance sheet might indicate that its investments, though large, were placed in foreign countries or in industries whose future was threatened. Other examples might, of course, be added at some length, all of them stressing the rather obvious point that of two complementary reports, neither alone will answer the purpose which the two together are designed to serve.

II. Current Capital Transactions

In the international financial statement as defined in the preceding section, no provision has been made for the presentation of data concerning what may be called current capital transactions. In short, there is no place in the balance sheet, nor in the income account, for classified data showing (1)

current investments in foreign securities and foreign enterprises, and various classes of direct loans to foreigners, or (2) sales to foreigners of domestic securities and of ownership in domestic enterprises, and the contraction of other foreign obligations. For a business concern, of course, such information is easily available from its bookkeeping records and is utilized in the compilation of the financial statement. It serves as a check against the income account, and is incorporated in the balance sheet as a component part of the classified totals presented there. But there is no set of books in which the international transactions of a country are recorded. Data pertaining to these must be compiled partly on the basis of recorded information, partly by statistical inference. If data are to be had concerning current capital transactions, therefore, their collection and presentation must be taken up for special consideration.

These data are needed in the compilation and checking of the income account and balance sheet. There is a very direct relationship between the capital transactions for a given period and the transactions recorded in the income account. These capital transactions, when summarized, show the amount by which net foreign assets or liabilities have increased or decreased during a period. The income account, on the other hand, explains this change. If the net international assets of Country A have increased during a given year by, say, a billion dollars, its surplus of international income for the year must likewise have amounted to a billion dollars. And if Country B, on the other hand, has experienced a certain net increase in its international liabilities, its deficiency of income must have amounted to exactly the same figure. If data concerning current capital transactions are collected, therefore, they furnish a check upon the income account. And, obviously, they are also very useful in the compilation of the balance sheet.

Data concerning capital transactions should be brought together in a report appended to the international financial state-

ment. The need for them is already well recognized—and considerable progress has been made in devising machinery for collecting them—but their usefulness and meaning is often obscured by the way in which they are presented.

For example, an investigator studying the accounts of Country A for a given period, finds that the import of commodities was met in part by the sacrifice of foreign securities. "Here," he says, "is an important factor that should not be overlooked." And with that he enters sales of securities as an item in the account he is compiling. Continuing his studies with infinite pains, he finds that of the credits granted to foreign buyers of A's exports, a certain net total is still outstanding at the end of the year. This item he also enters in his account. Like items follow. The final results of his systematic inquiry are thus presented all in one statement; and this statement, regardless of the name that may be given it, is nothing more than a trial balance covering all transactions for a given period.[13] So far, so good. A trial balance is a device useful in testing the completeness and accuracy of the data involved. It represents a preliminary step in the making of the final reports, but it should not be used as a substitute for those reports. Once the accuracy of the data has been established, the income and outgo items are transferred from it to the income account; data showing current capital transactions (changes in balance-sheet items) are incorporated in the balance sheet.

From an accounting point of view the data with regard to current capital transactions will thus have served their purpose and are no longer needed. But this does not follow in the case of the international accounts. The details concerning this large and important class of transactions have been brought together at the expense of a painstaking investigation. They are not matters of record in a set of "international books" kept concerning the foreign transactions carried on by the

[13] This point has already been referred to on pages 59-60 and 64.

government and people of a country. The balance sheet affords no place for recording them although a comparison of balance sheets will furnish a summary of them. There may be many cases, however, where these details would be of great help in connection with a particular problem. It therefore seems highly desirable that they should be brought together in a separate report to be presented along with the balance sheet and income account.[14]

III. Making the Reports Readable

The discussion thus far has been concerned with the problem of suiting the international financial reports to the broad purpose for which they are presented. But there is a further requirement to be met, namely, that they should be presented in such a way that the reader will have as little difficulty as possible in understanding the information they are intended to convey. Paraphrasing from a good accounting text: What shall it profit a statistician if he perform the highest grade of professional work and be unable to present the results in a form acceptable to and understandable by his public?

In making use of accounting terminology and forms, he must constantly bear in mind that the technical language of accounting is extremely difficult reading for the average person. Some accounting terms which mean much to the trained accountant, have little meaning for the uninitiated.

Much would be gained by foregoing the use of the words debit and credit. These terms are particularly confusing to those not well-grounded in accounting, and even the trained accountant often finds them hard to define and explain. Conventional usage has attached to each of them two apparently contradictory meanings. For example, in corporation accounting a debit to one of the accounts summarized in the income

[14] For a sample statement of current capital transactions see Chapter VII, p. 95.

account indicates an outgo or an expense of the business, while a debit to one of the accounts summarized in the balance sheet indicates an increase in that particular class of assets or a decrease in that particular class of liabilities. On the other hand, credit entries to the accounts summarized in the income account indicate receipts, or income, of the business, while credit entries to the accounts summarized in the balance sheet indicate a decrease in the particular classes of assets concerned or an increase in particular liabilities.

It will be seen that in the international financial statement, a debit balance in the income account means that international outgo has exceeded international income. This debit balance necessarily is offset by a credit balance in the account showing the capital (the loan and debt) transactions for the period; and a credit balance here means that the country has gone into debt or has parted with some of its claims against foreigners. On the other hand, a credit balance in the income account means that the operations for the period have produced an income surplus; while the offsetting debit balance in the account for "current capital transactions" indicates that foreign investments have increased or outstanding obligations to foreigners decreased.

In a "balance of payments" statement of the "trial balance" type the debits and credits are, of course, exactly equal. This is necessarily true, barring uncancelled errors in the data: one of the conventional rules, from which no exceptions are allowed in double entry bookkeeping, being that "every debit is exactly matched by a credit" and in consequence that "the sum of all the debits must equal the sum of all the credits." If some one item in the account is arbitrarily set out as the balancing item in the account, the terms "debit balance" or "credit balance" must be interpreted *as they relate to this particular account.* They have no meaning whatsoever as applied to the whole statement.

The quotation which follows shows what confusion may

result from the use of the terms debit and credit, particularly as applied to a "balance of payments" statement which does not distinguish clearly between trade and service operations and current capital transactions.

> Our balance of international payments for 1922 shows *that on the aggregate of its commercial and financial dealings with the world* this country had a large adverse balance. Total payments to foreign countries, on account of imports of merchandise and specie, purchases of foreign securities, immigrant's remittances, tourist expenditures, and other items representing payments of this country, exceeded total receipts from foreign countries by $586,000,000. This is the first year since the Armistice that a substantial debit has occurred in our international account; it is in striking contrast with 1919 and 1920, when the balance of payments showed a large surplus in our favor.[15]

The writer speaks of a "substantial debit" balance in an account which is said to include data for all classes of commercial and financial dealings. What can a "substantial debit" in such an account mean? Does it simply indicate the extent to which errors in the debit column are not cancelled out by errors in the credit column? The answer—which can be found only by a careful reading of many pages of the article—is that the amount of the floating debts or floating loans has been taken as the balancing item in the account, this having seemed the best way of arriving at an estimate for that item. A debit balance in the account as a whole would, therefore, indicate that there was a credit balance in the "ledger account" for floating debts and floating loans. To carry the interpretation further, the credit balance shown for this floating loans and debts account means one of two things: (1) either foreigners had reduced their short-term indebtedness to the United States, which is the probable explanation; or, (2) the people of the United States had increased the amount of their short-term

[15] *The Review of Economic Statistics*, Vol. V., 1923, p. 279. (Italics are mine.)

obligations to foreigners. In view of the huge accumulation of our loans to foreigners the reduction of any class of foreign loans should scarcely have been viewed with dissatisfaction. The fact that floating loans to foreigners were reduced is only part of the whole story, however. When the whole account for the year 1922 is analyzed (from the figures shown in the article quoted) it shows that, as a net result of the year's operations, foreigners owed the United States 52 million dollars less at the end of the year than at the beginning, a condition of affairs which is in no way indicated by the quotation.

The report in question could have been saved from ambiguity if its interpretation had been put into simple, understandable language.[16] And this matter of interpretation would have been easier if (1) the income account and the statement of current capital transactions had been presented as two separate reports, and (2) if the terms debit and credit had been discarded in favor of more meaningful words.

The arrangement of items in the account may be used to help simplify its meaning. Accountants have devised and make use of a variety of forms for presenting the items in both the balance sheet and the income account. No one of them, of course, can ever be designated as *the best;* for that which is best for one purpose may be poor for another. As a whole they divide into two broad classes, to which the terms "account form" and "report form" are applied.

In the "account form" of statement the items are set forth in two parallel columns, the column on the left headed "debits," and the column on the right headed "credits."[17] The report

[16] The headings which the League of Nations uses for the two main divisions of its report form (see Chapter VI, pp. 79-82) also show how difficult it is to make clear the meaning of the terms debit and credit. One of these two divisions is headed "Inward or Credit Movements (Exports)," and the other, "Outward or Debit Movements (Imports)."

[17] In presenting the balance sheet in account form, it is customary to put the liabilities on the right hand or credit side, and the assets on the left hand or debit side. Practice in England, however, is just the

form of balance sheet shows the assets grouped together with the liabilities items grouped below them. The report form of income statement shows income, expenditures, and the net difference between the two *for each class* of transactions covered by the report. It thus summarizes the various transactions in the form of a running story that is fairly easily read.

For the uninitiated the report form of statement is preferable, for it helps interpret the data that it gives. The "account form" of statement on the other hand—which gives the "debits" for each class of transactions in one column, and the offsetting credits in the other,—leaves the reader to make his own calculations and interpretations concerning the net result of each class of operations. The fact that in the "report" form the troublesome words "debit" and "credit" may be dispensed with, and the net results for each class of transactions may be set down in readable English—for example, net income from shipping, net outgo for tourists' expenditures, etc.—particularly recommends this form of statements for use in the international financial accounts.

reverse of this: liabilities are entered at the left under the heading of debits, and assets are entered on the right under the heading of credits. (See Hatfield, H. R., *Accounting*, 1927, pp. 5, 53, and 57, and the 1913 ed., pp. 41-45.) This lack of uniformity argues against the use of the "account form" in the presentation of the international accounts. It may be noted that here is an additional argument against the use of the words "debit" and "credit" in connection with these accounts.

CHAPTER VI

CURRENT USAGE EXEMPLIFIED

Preceding chapters have shown that the international financial statements of a country would more completely answer their purpose if they were patterned after the financial statements used in the field of business. What would be involved in adopting this pattern can probably best be shown by presenting some of the types of international financial statements now in use and comparing these with current usage in the field of business. For illustrative types our choice falls upon the Board of Trade Journal reports for Great Britain, the standard form suggested by the League of Nations, and the form of report now used by the Department of Commerce of the United States.

I. British Board of Trade Journal Statement

In 1919 the Board of Trade Journal began the practice of publishing, early each year, a special article on the subject of the "Balance of Trade." Under this heading outstanding facts concerning the international trade and service transactions of the country for the preceding year are discussed and compared with those for earlier years. The data presented are then brought together in table form, followed by an interpretation of the table as a whole and of its relation to the question of the foreign trade of the United Kingdom (Great Britain and Northern Ireland).

The report form that has been adopted for presenting these data is given below, reproduced from the January 27, 1927, issue of the *Journal*.

BALANCES OF INCOME AND EXPENDITURES IN THE TRANSACTIONS
(other than lending and repayment of capital)
BETWEEN THE UNITED KINGDOM AND ALL OTHER COUNTRIES

Particulars	1924	1925	1926
	In Million £'s		
Excess of Imports of Merchandise and Bullion...	324	384	477
Estimated Excess of Government Payments Made Overseas[1]	25	11	...
Total	349	395	477
Estimated Net National Shipping Income[2]	140	124	120
Estimated Net Income from Overseas Investments	220	250	270
Estimated Receipts from Short Interest and Commissions	60	60	60
Estimated Receipts from Other Services	15	15	15
Total	435	449	465
Estimated Total Credit (+) or Debit (−) Balance on Items Specified Above	+ 86	+ 54	− 12

[1] These include some items on loan accounts.
[2] Including disbursements of foreign ships in British ports.

In the terminology of corporation accounting, this is essentially an income statement.[1] It shows the net amount available from current income, or current revenue transactions, for increasing foreign investment or decreasing foreign debts. It will be seen that for two of the items in the account the outgo of the country is greater than the income. These are the first two items, "Excess of imports of merchandise and bullion" and "Estimated excess of government payments made overseas." For all other classes of transactions itemized, income exceeded outgo. Total net outgo for the first two classes

[1] One exception should be noted. The item "Excess of government payments made overseas" includes along with certain income and outgo on government account, the amounts paid out and received on the principal of the foreign loans and debts of the government. On this score the *Journal* says: ". . . receipts and payments by the British Government on account of inter-governmental loans have been included . . . because they originate in the State revenue of the year, and, anyhow, are not large enough to disturb the figures." (January 21, 1926, p. 70.)

of transactions is subtracted from total net income from the other items, and the balance for each year is indicated at the bottom of the column.

The *Journal* gives warning that the reader of the table should allow for a certain margin of error in the estimates set forth, and has indicated the limits within which figures showing the true "balance," if it could be determined for each year, would probably lie. Substituting these for the precise results presented in the table, the statement shows that Great Britain had net income of about 75 to 100 million pounds sterling available for new investments abroad in 1924; between 40 and 80 millions in 1925; while in 1926 she probably fell slightly short of having income sufficient to meet all current obligations.

The Journal does not present a statement of current capital transactions. If such a statement had been drawn up it would have furnished a check upon the results set forth in the income account, and thus would have roughly confirmed its accuracy or would have led to its revision. For, when all items are taken into consideration, the net change in a country's foreign debt and investment position must check exactly with its net income or net outgo on trade and service account. This point has been discussed at some length on pages 65-69. The *Journal's* income statement for 1926, which shows outgo slightly in excess of income, leads unavoidably to the conclusion that in 1926 Great Britain had parted with some of her investments, long or short-term, or else had borrowed in foreign markets. But details concerning all classes of borrowing and lending operations are not available.

In the absence of a corroborating statement showing capital transactions for the year, British bank reviews and financial papers in general have been inclined to question the accuracy of the *Journal's* income statement, rather than to accept these conclusions. It has been contended by numerous writers that such investment data as are available lead to a directly oppo-

site conclusion. The *Journal's* estimate of the international income of the country and the data with reference to new investments appear on the face of things to be contradictory—which leads the *Statist* to remark that "it is easier to explain away the statistics than to explain the paradoxical conclusion they would indicate." [2]

The difficulty with the data that have been presented with reference to capital transactions is that they give information for only one class of transactions, namely, new long-term investments. Such figures do not by any means show the actual *net* amount of new investments, as the *Journal* itself points out:

> Foreigners are constantly buying British and other securities on London, sometimes to considerable amounts, and London is always buying foreign and home securities from abroad, and on balance there may be funds available for new investment. Short-term foreign money has been on occasion largely placed in London, and with the recovery of London as an international financial centre it is probable that foreign balances are larger than they were some years ago, but, although while they were growing they helped us to finance overseas loans, obviously this effect is not recurrent. A third source of funds for overseas investment is that of sinking funds for overseas loans, which certainly amount to a considerable sum. On account of these capital transactions, as well as for reasons which have been expounded at length in previous annual reviews, there is no reason for expecting a close correspondence between the total of new overseas issues offered on the London market in any year and the available balances of national income, and, accordingly, the excess of such issues over balances is no evidence that the latter are seriously under-estimated.[3]

The *Journal* thus rightly argues that the one item, "new overseas issues," is altogether inadequate for the purpose of testing the accuracy of its income account. Such a test can be

[2] January 15, 1927, p. 79.

[3] *Board of Trade Journal*, January 27, 1927, p. 93.

furnished only by a statement which includes estimates for all capital transactions of all classes.[4] It is evident from these British discussions that the need for reliable data showing current changes in the international debt and investment position of the country is clearly recognized.

No thorough investigation covering international balance sheet items has been made for Great Britain since the war. The *Journal* apparently has made a very rough estimate of the net total of Britain's foreign investments, but is unwilling to risk its publication. On several occasions, it has pointed out that the estimates given concerning the interest item in the account are based on the calculations made by Sir George Paish in 1909 and 1911, and that these have really ceased to be applicable in the circumstances of the post-war world. Because of this lack of balance sheet data, as they point out, the interest item in the account is a very rough estimate indeed, being perhaps as much as 20 per cent below or above the net amount actually accruing to Great Britain.

The *Journal,* no less than its critics, deplores its lack of information, saying that "It is much to be regretted that no separate study of this immensely important subject has been made by British bankers, who must have at their disposal a considerable stock of information."[5] Thus the bankers turn to the official organ of the Board of Trade, asking for an explanation of the present situation of Great Britain, and it in turn appeals to them.

Of the three sets of reports which it would be desirable to have, it will be seen that the *Journal* gives only one, the

[4] The Midland Bank, with a view to checking the reliability of the income data, has made a hasty survey of all classes of long and short-term transactions in which the people of Great Britain might have engaged. It is of interest to note that these rough estimates of capital movements cast doubt upon, rather than confirmed, the *Journal's* estimates. (*Monthly Review* of the Midland Bank Limited, October-November, 1926.)

[5] *Board of Trade Journal,* January 21, 1926, p. 69.

income account. And for want of the other two, the statement of current capital transactions and the balance sheet, the one that it does present is coming to be regarded as of little practical significance.

II. League of Nations Report Form

Impressed with the importance of having available as accurate data as possible on the international accounts of various countries, the League of Nations, as we have said, has undertaken the work of bringing together and publishing these accounts for all countries willing to co-operate. Each year the League statisticians urgently request all governments to send in their annual financial statements covering the international transactions of their respective countries. To make the reports for different countries as nearly comparable as possible, they have worked out a form of report that they tentatively recommend be used by all. To illustrate the standard form of report now used for this purpose the statement for the Union of South Africa is given below, as it appeared in the *Memorandum* published by the League late in 1926.[6]

Union of South Africa, 1924

Inward or Credit Movements (Exports)	£ (000's)	
	Amounts	Sub-totals and Total
I. *Merchandise*		
1. Merchandise exported (as per trade returns)	40,122	
2. Adjustment for under- or over-valuation of (1) in order to arrive at the commercial value f.o.b.	.....	
3. Contraband	.....	40,122

[6] It is the purpose of the League statisticians to revise and improve this standard report form in the light of suggestions and criticisms made by the statisticians of the various countries.

UNION OF SOUTH AFRICA, 1924—*Continued*

INWARD OR CREDIT MOVEMENTS (Exports)	£ (000's) Amounts	£ (000's) Sub-totals and Total
II. *Bullion, specie, and currency notes*		
4. Gold bullion and specie exported (as per trade returns)	44,261	
5. Silver bullion and specie exported (as per trade returns)	52	
6. Currency notes	.....	
7. Adjustment for under- or over-valuation of (4) and (5) in order to arrive at the commercial value f.o.b.	– 1,208	43,105
III. *Capital Items*		
8. Receipt of payments on account of amortisation of foreign Government and municipal loans	.....	
9. Receipt of payments on account of amortisation of other loans	.....	
10. Existing domestic securities sold abroad	.....	
11. Foreign securities resold abroad	250	
12. Export of new domestic securities on account of new loans floated abroad	5,409	
13. Domestic real estate sold to foreigners	.....	
14. Other foreign capital invested in South Africa	1,360	7,019
IV. *Interest and Dividends*		
15. Interest received on foreign Government and municipal loans	145	
16. Other interest and dividends received from capital invested abroad	.....	145
V. *Other Items*		
17. Shipping freights, charter money, passage money and similar earnings received by national ships on accounts of all foreign trade	.....	
18. Port receipts from foreign shipping in national ports	537	
19. Transport and other charges received for foreign goods transhipped or in transit	195	
20. Commissions, insurance, brokerage and similar receipts	.....	
21. Post and telegraph earnings	.....	
22. Funds brought in by immigrants and returned emigrants	.....	

UNION OF SOUTH AFRICA, 1924—*Continued*

INWARD OR CREDIT MOVEMENTS (Exports)	£ (000's)	
	Amounts	Sub-totals and Total
23. Emigrants' remittances and money gifts from abroad. Pensions paid by Imperial Government	568	
24. Receipts from foreign tourists and travellers	609	
25. Diplomatic, consular and similar expenditure in Union of South Africa	340	
26. Receipts for services rendered in Union of South Africa for "persons" domiciled abroad	.....	
27. Government receipts from abroad, not elsewhere indicated	127	
28. Other current items	.....	2,376
Total		92,767

OUTWARD OR DEBIT MOVEMENTS (Imports)	£ (000's)	
	Amounts	Sub-totals and Total
I. *Merchandise*		
29. Merchandise imported (as per trade returns)	65,816	
30. Adjustment for under- or over-valuation of (29) in order to arrive at the commercial value c.i.f.		
Freight and Insurance:		
(a)	5,128	
(b)	− 1,606	
31. Contraband	....	69,338
II. *Bullion, specie, and currency notes*		
32. Gold bullion and specie imported (as per trade returns)	.....	
33. Silver bullion and specie imported (as per trade returns)	79	

UNION OF SOUTH AFRICA, 1924—*Continued*

OUTWARD OR DEBIT MOVEMENTS (Imports)	£ (000's) Amounts	Sub-totals and Total
34. Currency notes	.....	
35. Adjustment for under- or over-valuation of (32) and (33) in order to arrive at the commercial value c.i.f.	.....	79
III. *Capital Items*		
....	.....	.....
IV. *Interest and Dividends*		
36. Interest paid on Government and municipal foreign debt	5,301	
37. Interest and dividends paid on foreign capital invested in South Africa	11,821	17,122
V. *Other Items*		
38. Shipping freights, charter money, passage money and similar earnings paid to foreign ships on account of all home and foreign trade other than imports into Union of South Africa	.....	
39. Port expenses incurred by national shipping in foreign ports	.....	
40. Transport payments to foreign carriers ..	260	
41. Commission, insurance, brokerage and similar payments	1,285	
42. Post and telegraph payments	92	
43. Funds taken out by emigrants and returning immigrants	720	
44. Immigrants' remittances and money gifts sent abroad	.....	
45. Expenditure abroad by national tourists and travellers	4,267	
46. Diplomatic, consular and similar expenditure abroad	156	
47. Payments for services rendered abroad for "persons" domiciled in Union of South Africa	.....	
48. Government expenditure abroad not indicated elsewhere	215	
49. Other current items	.....	6,995
Total		93,534
BALANCE (increase or decrease in floating indebtedness)		— 767

SUMMARY TABLE

	£ (000's)		
	Credit	Debit	Balance
I. Merchandise	40,122	69,338	− 29,216
II. Bullion, specie and currency notes	43,105	79	+ 43,026
III. Capital items	7,019	.....	+ 7,019
IV. Interest and dividends	145	17,122	− 16,977
V. Other items	2,376	6,995	− 4,619
Total	92,767	93,534	
Balance			− 767[a]

[a] To make the "balance" column balance, the sign should be plus.

This statement gives income-account data and data for capital transactions but does not separate the one class from the other. All credit items, whether they represent the export of commodities, income from services performed for foreigners, receipts from new long-term borrowings abroad, or receipts from the sale of foreign securities belonging to the people of the Union of South Africa, are put together under the heading "Inward or Credit movements (Exports)." Likewise, all debit items, whether they represent imports of commodities, outgo for services rendered by foreigners, new long-term loans granted to foreigners, or foreign debts paid off by the nation, are grouped together under the heading "Outward or Debit Movements (Imports)."

The items under each of these main headings are divided into five sub-classes. Under the sub-title "Capital items" are itemized the various classes of transactions which have made for changes one way or the other in the international assets and liabilities of the country. With some emendations, the two sets of estimates grouped under this sub-title, give the data required for drawing up a statement of current capital transactions. The other four classes of items included in each of the two large groups are, in the main, items representing income

or outgo. To arrive at an estimate of the net results of short-term borrowing and lending transactions for the year, it is assumed that this class of transactions represent the balancing item in the account.

As the table is presented, the reader must recombine the figures given if he is to find the net results of the year's international transactions. When he has arrived at an interpretation of each of the five classes of items given in the table and has taken note of the balancing item set forth, he must summarize the data to find the net deficit or surplus from trade and service operations for the year; and also to find the net results of borrowing and lending operations. Apparently the summary table given at the end of the detailed table has been included for the purpose of obviating this necessity. But the summary table, as well as the detailed table, fails to separate trade and service transactions into a group clearly distinguished from capital transactions. This task is left to the reader. However, as we shall see, when the reader attempts to use the summary table as a basis for recombining the data, he will find that it also is a source of some confusion.

In the detailed table the balancing item, "increase or decrease in floating indebtedness," is shown on the debit side as "—767." A negative item on the debit side of an account is, of course, equal to a positive item on the credit side. And a credit item, when it is applied to changes in the debt or investment standing of a country, represents either a net decrease in outstanding loans, or a net increase in debts. From its wording, we may assume that the present item represents an increase in the floating indebtedness of the Union of South Africa—rather than a decrease in its short-term loans to foreigners.[8]

[7] We say "in the main" because there is one exception which will be discussed later; see pp. 86-88.

[8] If a balance sheet were available showing the debt and investment standing of the Union of South Africa for the end of 1923, there would, of course, be no difficulty in interpreting this item.

This item of "—767" (representing increased floating indebtedness) is carried over from the detailed table into the summary table. Instead of being entered in the column headed "debit," however, it is entered in the "balance" column, the entry apparently being intended to bring the balance column into balance. But as a matter of fact it does not establish a balance unless the sign is changed to plus. The confusion may perhaps be more clearly seen by noting that an increase in the long-term indebtedness of the country is indicated by a plus sign, while an increase in floating indebtedness is shown by the minus sign.

To ascertain the net result of the year's operations, therefore, it is necessary, in the summary table, to change the sign of the balancing item from a minus to a plus; and in both the detailed and the summary tables it is necessary to recombine the results for the various classes of items set forth.

If income-account items were separated from those showing current capital transactions, the statement would tell a clear-cut story. And incidentally, the difficulties involved in the use of the troublesome words debit and credit might be obviated. To show what is involved in breaking up the statement in this way, the items given in the summary table are reclassified on page 86. If it were desired, the detailed statement given on pages 79-82 might also be re-arranged in a similar fashion.

The table on page 86 shows the reader at a glance the net results of all international transactions for the single year 1924. The country's net income from gold exports fell 7,786 thousand pounds short of satisfying outgo requirements. This deficit was met by foreign borrowings, by the investment of foreign funds in South African enterprises, or by the sale to foreigners of South African holdings of foreign securities .

If the detailed statement had been re-arranged in this way into an itemized income account and an itemized statement of current capital transactions, it would have been necessary to have broken up the items shown (on pages 80-82) under the

TRADE AND SERVICE ACCOUNT OF THE UNION OF SOUTH AFRICA, 1924
(In thousands of pounds sterling)

NET INCOME FROM—			
Bullion and specie:			
Exports	43,105		
Less imports	79		43,026
NET OUTGO FOR—			
Merchandise:			
Imports	69,338		
Less exports	40,122	29,216	
Interest and dividends:			
Income	145		
Outgo	17,122	16,977	
Other service items:			
Income	2,376		
Outgo	6,995	4,619	50,812
Net deficit on trade and service account			7,786

Capital Transactions of the Union of South Africa, 1924
(In thousands of pounds sterling)

RECEIPTS (from new borrowings, or from the sale of foreign securities)	
Long-term operations	7,019
Short-term operations	767
Net receipts from borrowing, available for meeting the trade and service deficit	7,786

sub-title "bullion, specie, and currency notes." Some of these items, as a matter of fact, belong in the income account, some in the statement of capital transactions. The items showing imports and exports of bullion and specie belong in the income account. The two items showing purchases and sales of currency notes (items 6 and 34) indicate changes in the foreign assets and liabilities of the country. These statements may require some explanation.

Purchases and sales of bullion and specie are transactions that should be entered in the income account. The reason for this is fairly clear. The *international* balance sheet of a country includes only two broad classes of items: (1) claims against foreigners, and (2) obligations to foreigners. Gold belongs in neither of these two classes. In the trade between countries it is a commodity that must be taken account of

like any other commodity. Giffen pointed this out very emphatically:

> . . . In the trade of England the precious metals are exactly in the position of any other commodity. Like oils and seeds and other articles of raw produce, gold and silver are brought into this country from the places where they are produced, are smelted, assayed, and treated here like many other commodities, and the products are then distributed over the world, the trade in the precious metals being thus a trade like any other.[9]

As distinguished from the items that appear in the international balance sheet, it does not represent a *claim* against any particular country, though it is a commodity generally acceptable by all.[10]

The item "currency notes," on the other hand, is a capital item. Currency notes are credit instruments. Aside from the promise to pay which they represent they have little if any value. In rare cases, repudiated currency notes have been known to have served as wall covering, but for such purpose they excited little demand. Unless they have been repudiated, currency notes of country A, if in the hands of residents of country B, represent a non-interest bearing foreign obligation of country A payable on demand. The holder in country B may, at his pleasure, demand from country A either goods, gold, or services in exchange for this paper. And until it has been redeemed, through some trade or service transaction, country A must stand ready to meet the demands that the holder in country B may make. In this respect, currency notes in the hands of a foreign holder do not differ from stocks, bonds, and other forms of domestic securities held by foreigners.

[9] Giffen, Sir Robert, *Statistics*, p. 70.

[10] It must be remembered that the balance sheet of which we speak here is the balance sheet of the nation considered as a foreign trading corporation. It is the international balance sheet. The *consolidated* balance sheet of the nation showing total national wealth of *all* classes, would, of course, include gold among the assets.

International purchases and sales of currency notes—whether domestic or foreign—therefore, should be entered in the statement showing current capital transactions.

In the League of Nations statement, the international balance sheet is omitted. The inclusion of a debt and investment, or balance sheet, statement for each of the several countries represented in the League's *Memorandum* would, of course, be highly desirable, and probably is upon the future program of the League statisticians. At the present time, wherever such data are offered by the various countries, they are published. For example, the *Memorandum* covering the years 1911-1925 gives balance sheet data for Denmark in summary form for a long period of years. The difficulty involved in the collection of these data for all countries has, however, probably argued against any general effort to secure them at the present time.

III. Department of Commerce Statement

The Department of Commerce of the United States has been working for some time on the problem of improving both the data that are included in the international accounts of the United States, and the form in which these data are presented. The form of account used in presenting the reports for 1925 is given on page 89. It will be seen that it differs in some respects from the two that have already been discussed.

A slight re-arrangement of the statement would be required to bring it into agreement with current business practice. From a cursory reading it will be seen that the account divides into two large classes of items: "current items" and "movements of capital." The line describing the total of all items listed under the heading of current items reads: "total current items other than gold and silver," thus indicating that gold and silver are, in fact, classified as "current items." Changes in foreign bank deposits, of course, clearly belong in

ESTIMATED BALANCE OF INTERNATIONAL PAYMENTS OF THE UNITED STATES, 1925*

[Millions of dollars]

Items	Exports (credits)	Imports (debits)	Balance
CURRENT ITEMS			
Visible current items:			
Merchandise	4,934 [a]	4,268 [b]	+ 666
Invisible current items:			
Interest on inter-Ally debt	160	....	+ 160
Private interest and dividends	520	165	+ 355
Ocean freights	75	83	− 8
Governmental payments	....	5	− 5
Services to tourists	100	660	− 560
Charitable and missionary expenditures	....	50	− 50
Immigrants' remittances	....	310	− 310
Motion-picture royalties	75	....	+ 75
Total, invisible current items	930	1,273	− 343
Total, current items other than gold and silver	5,864	5,541	+ 323
MOVEMENTS OF CAPITAL			
New foreign loans, exclusive of refunding	....	920	− 920
Sale and purchase of outstanding securities	411	90	+ 321
Foreign bonds paid off	140	....	+ 140
Principal of inter-Ally debt	27	....	+ 27
United States paper currency	....	62	− 62
Total, capital items	578	1,072	− 494
GOLD AND SILVER			
Gold	262	128	+ 134
Silver	99	65	+ 34
Total, gold and silver	361	193	+ 168
Total, all items	6,803	6,806	− 3
Change in foreigners' bank deposits, as revealed by questionnaire	....	....	− 61
Residual balance (representing errors and omissions)			− 64

* Trade Information Bulletin 399, p. 3.

[a] Includes $25,000,000 for unrecorded parcel-post packages.

[b] Includes $40,000,000 for smuggled goods.

the "movements of capital" group.[11] Items classed as "current items" are in fact income and outgo items. Those dubbed "movements of capital" are well named, representing, as they do, what we have called the current capital transactions for the period.

Now, if the figures showing gold and silver imports and exports were added into the total for other current items, the resulting figures would show total income and total outgo for the year, as well as net income or outgo for each item. Total income for the year 1925 would thus be shown at a figure of 6,225 million dollars; total outgo at 5,734 millions. The net income of the country on all trade and service accounts would thus approximate 491 million dollars.

This net income must, of course, be reflected in the debt and investment statement of the country in one of two ways. It may account for an increase in the international assets of the United States; that is, in a net increase in foreign loans. Or, it may explain decreases in the international liabilities (foreign debts) of the United States.

To find how the various classes of international assets and liabilities of the country were affected by the year's operations, we look at the group of items designated "movements of capital." Here, as in the League of Nations statement, the column headings make these items somewhat difficult to interpret. A net increase of foreign loans and foreign investments is indicated in the "balance" column with a minus sign, and the same is true of the net increase in foreign bank deposits. This is mathematically correct, but nevertheless is unnecessarily con-

[11] The text that accompanies this table indicates, however, that the writer did not comprehend the difference between the balance sheet and the income account, for he says: "All of our exports and imports may be divided into two great classes—current items and capital items. The distinction between the two groups is based largely upon the length of time they remain in existence. and corresponds roughly to the business man's distinction between current assets and fixed assets. . . ." *Trade Information Bulletin,* 399, p. 1.

fusing to the reader. Including this increase in foreign bank deposits along with other capital items, the account shows that the total of all loans (exclusive of commercial credits on open account) granted by the United States to foreigners increased during the year by a net amount of 555 million dollars.

Thus on the one hand the country's net income for the year totalled 491 million dollars on the other, the net increase in foreign loans, or foreign investments, amounted to 555 million dollars. The difference between these two figures, 64 million dollars, is according to a statement made in the *Bulletin* (page 2) a "residual balance (representing errors and omissions)."

A complete balance sheet is not given. The "assets" or investments side of the balance sheet (with the exception of floating credits) is given in the form reproduced on page 92.[12] No estimate is given, however, of the international "liabilities" of the people of the United States, the total of which must amount to a considerable sum.

A corporation financial statement which showed assets alone, with no indication of the amount of offsetting liabilities, would be considered entirely inadequate for the general purposes for which financial statements are required. The same is true of the international financial statement which shows the foreign investments of a country, but leaves out offsetting foreign debts. If the balance sheet were complete—if floating credits were included among the foreign investments, and if the foreign obligations of the states, corporations, and citizens of the country were shown—the international financial statement published by the Department of Commerce would be very nearly in accord with accounting standards that are met in the field of business.

[12] This table indicates that American investments abroad increased by 1,125 million dollars in 1924; and by 1,175 millions in 1925. The data given under the heading of "capital items" does not check with this figure, however. In corporation accounting such a check would be required.

Estimated Value of American Investments Abroad at End of Calendar Years 1923, 1924, and 1925 *

[Millions of dollars]

Regions	Government guaranteed obligations	Industrial securities and direct investments	Total
At end of 1923 (revised):			
Europe	950	350	1,300
Latin America	610	3,150	3,760
Canada and Newfoundland	1,050	1,400	2,450
Asia, Australia, Africa, and rest of world	360	235	595
Total	2,670	5,485	8,105
At end of 1924 (revised):			
Europe	1,500	400	1,900
Latin America	840	3,200	4,040
Canada and Newfoundland	1,100	1,500	2,600
Asia, Australia, Africa, and rest of world	440	250	690
Total	3,880	5,350	9,230
At end of 1925:			
Europe	1,825	675	2,500
Latin America	910	3,300	4,210
Canada and Newfoundland	1,175	1,650	2,825
Asia, Australia, Africa, and rest of world	520	350	870
Total	4,430	5,975	10,405

* *Trade Information Bulletin*, No. 399, p. 15.

Measured by the standards set in business, it will be seen that all three of the statements presented above are open to certain criticisms. Some data that it would be desirable to have are missing. A clearer presentation of the data that are included would be helpful to the reader. And yet, these statements show a decided improvement over current usage of a decade ago. The fact that they are compiled annually is a matter of great practical importance. And their inclusion of data with regard to current capital transactions is a post-war development that promises much for the future.

CHAPTER VII

A SAMPLE STATEMENT

To illustrate the way in which the financial statement used in business may be adapted to the requirements of international finance, this chapter will present a sample statement summarizing the hypothetical accounts of any given country. The purpose is to show in a concrete way the relationship existing between the various separate reports that make up the complete statement, rather than to urge the advantages to be gained by any particular arrangement of items within the several reports. In the discussion of the statement, some general questions of definition are raised for consideration. A survey of the data now available for compiling such statements is left to Chapter VIII.

1. The Statement

During the year 1926, let us say, the people of country X carried on a variety of trade and service transactions with the rest of the world, in the course of which they incurred new foreign obligations and accumulated new foreign assets. To give a complete story of these various operations and to show their effect upon the international financial position of X, the statement for the year must contain, according to the analysis of Chapter V, (1) an income account, (2) a statement of current capital transactions, (3) a comparative balance sheet, showing the country's international debt and investment position at the beginning and end of the year.

The hypothetical income account showing the international trade and service transactions of X for the year 1926 is as follows:

INCOME ACCOUNT OF X
(Showing trade and service transactions for 1926)

	In millions of specified monetary units		
NET INCOME FROM—			
Merchandise:			
Exports	250.2		
Less imports	210.0	40.2	
Gold and silver coin and bullion:			
Exports	.8		
Less imports	.5	.3	
Commissions, insurance, etc.		2.5	
Shipping freights, charter money, passenger money, etc. (including net income from port charges)		11.0	
Railway receipts from the transit trade		1.0	
Post, telegraph, and telephone earnings		1.0	
Tourist trade:			
Receipts from foreign tourists and travellers	26.0		
Less expenditures by nationals travelling abroad	3.0	23.0	
Diplomatic and consular services, etc.:			
Expenditures of foreign officials in X	4.0		
Less expenditures abroad by officials of X	1.8	2.2	
Emigrants' remittances		2.0	83.2
NET OUTGO FOR—			
Interest:			
On inter-governmental loans and debts:			
Outgo	1.0		
Less income	.5	.5	
On securities of governments, states, municipalities, etc., privately held:			
Outgo	10.6		
Less income	5.3	5.3	
On other securities, and on direct investments:			
Outgo	17.5		
Less income	4.5	13.0	18.8
Net surplus from trade and service operations (available for investment abroad, or for the reduction of foreign debts)			64.4

A detailed analysis of changes in the debt and investment position of X during the year is set forth in the statement of current capital transactions which follows. It will be seen that the figure for net outlay on capital account shown by this

statement checks exactly with the figure for net surplus in the income account.

CAPITAL TRANSACTIONS OF X FOR THE YEAR 1926

	In millions of specified monetary units			
RECEIPTS:				
Borrowings from foreigners—				
Borrowings of X government from other governments		20.0		
Foreign borrowings of railways and corporations		2.0	22.0	
Decrease in deposits in foreign banks			.5	
Sale of foreign currency			.5	23.0
OUTGO:				
Loans to foreigners—				
Loans by X government to foreign governments		15.0		
Private investment in new securities of foreign governments, states, and municipalities, issued in X	5.0			
Less discounts on bond issues ...	.1	4.9		
Private investment in foreign corporation securities, issued in X	8.0			
Less discounts on bond issues ...	.4	7.6		
Purchase of outstanding securities of foreign corporations	2.0			
Less discounts	.1	1.9	29.4	
Repurchase from foreigners of the currency notes of X		15.0		
Repurchase of domestic securities held abroad—				
Issues of the government of X		10.0		
Issues of domestic corporations, etc., of X		20.0	30.0	
Repayment of commercial loans			13.0	87.4
Net outgo, representing the net reduction of foreign claims against X				64.4

The figures showing net changes in the several classes of international assets and liabilities, once they have been brought together and set forth in the statement of current capital transactions, are then used in the compilation of the closing balance sheet. Below is given the comparative balance sheet for X, showing the country's international debt and investment position at the close of 1926 as compared with that for the close of 1925.

Comparative International Balance Sheet of X *

Showing debt and investment position at close of 1925 and 1926
(In millions of specified monetary units)

	December 31, 1925		December 31, 1926	
INVESTMENTS:				
Private investment in securities of foreign governments, states, and municipalities	100		105	
Private investment in foreign corporation securities	40		50	
Direct ownership in foreign enterprises (including real estate), and mortgages on foreign property	50		50	
Holdings of foreign currency notes	5		4.5	
Total deposits (time and demand) with foreigners	5		4.5	
Bank loans and advances (including overdrafts) to foreigners	5		5	
Short-term investments abroad (including all bills and short term securities)	5		5	
Commercial credits (on open account, promissory notes, etc.)	5		5	
Government loans of X to foreign governments	10		25	
		225		254
DEBTS:				
Foreign holdings of the national, state, and municipal securities of X	210		200	
Foreign holdings of securities of X corporations	250		232	
Direct ownership by foreigners in the enterprises of X (including real estate), and foreign mortgages on domestic property of X	100		100	
Total deposits (time and demand) of foreigners with the banks of X	3		3	
Bank loans and advances (including overdrafts) due to foreigners	6		6	
Foreigners' investments in short-term securities (including all bills and short-term Treasury securities) of X	6		6	
Commercial debts (on open account, promissory notes, etc.)	50		37	
Currency notes issued by X and held abroad	50		35	
Government debts owed by X to foreign governments	10		30	
		685		649
NET TOTAL of foreign debts, in excess of foreign investments		460		395

CONTINGENT LIABILITIES: In case of a default by country A of its debt to country B, country X is liable for 20 per cent of the whole amount (state the amount of the liability), country X having guaranteed 20 per cent of this loan.

* It is suggested on p. 66 that for various purposes it is desirable to have a geographic classification of loans and investments, and also to have long-term debts and investments classified to show whether they are public or private obligations, and by what types of industries the private obligations had been incurred. The classification to show geographic distribution and distribution by industries would probably best be given in appended tables rather than in the balance sheet proper.

It will be seen that there is an apparent discrepancy between the comparative balance sheet, which shows that the net reduction in foreign obligations amounted to 65, and the statement of current capital transactions, which shows that net outgo for the reduction of foreign obligations amounted to 64.4. The explanation is that the statement of current capital transactions indicates the net outgo for new loans issued in X, after deductions had been made for discounts, while the balance sheet gives the nominal value of the loans.[1]

An item-by-item comparison of the data given in the statement of current capital transactions and in the two columns of the comparative balance sheet, indicates the way in which the balance sheet figures for the end of the year were obtained. Increases and decreases in the figures for the various classes of claims against foreigners and obligations to foreigners were transferred directly from the statement of current capital transactions to the balance sheet. This method of adjusting the balance sheet items obviates the necessity for making a detailed study of the complete balance sheet each time the financial statement is drawn up. However, in order to make the accounts as nearly accurate as possible, it is highly desirable that an additional check on these balance sheet data should be made periodically. For this purpose an independent estimate of the balance sheet items is practically necessary.

The compilation of data for this additional check on the balance-sheet would doubtless require the taking of a complete census covering all classes of foreign debts and investments outstanding at a given date. This would, of course, be an ex-

[1] It might perhaps be argued that discounts should be shown in the income account, rather than in the statement of current capital transactions. On the other hand, the history of international borrowing and lending operations shows that the discount item may sometimes loom very large, and would sometimes greatly distort the income account if included there; whereas if included in the statement of current capital transactions it gives information very useful in interpreting that account. See discussion of discounts and premiums, pp. 102-104.

tremely difficult task, however it were handled. It could scarcely be accomplished without the co-operation of the big banks, and investment houses, and of importers and exporters of goods; and also, it is doubtful whether anything but a rough approximation could be secured for many years to come. It is therefore quite likely that the taking of such a census should not be attempted oftener than say once in every five or ten years. For intervening years, the balance sheet data could be obtained by the method followed in the sample statement above.[2]

Until the methods for taking such a census had been perfected, the resulting balance sheet would probably give only a very rough check on the income accounts and balance sheet data available for preceding years. It is also quite likely that the results of such a census would have to be revised somewhat in the light of data that had previously been collected and used in the compilation of the annual financial statements for preceding years.

Incidentally, it may be said that so far as the United States is concerned, the studies published in the *Review of Economic Statistics* and in the annual reports of the Department of Commerce give most of the data that would be required for drawing up rough balance sheets for various dates from about 1818 down to the present time. The approximate net total of the country's foreign debts in 1818 is known, and is given in these studies along with the income account data, and data concerning current capital transactions for subsequent years. These are the data from which the balance sheets might be constructed. Such balance sheets, however, should be subjected to a thorough scrutiny, in the light of all data available

[2] The questionnaire used by the U. S. Department of Commerce in collecting information concerning current capital transactions is given in Appendix B, pp. 163-165; and the questionnaire used by the French government in its census of French investments abroad, 1902, is given in Appendix A, pp. 143-144.

concerning the years under consideration. As one means of checking the data for later years, a census of the sort suggested above should be taken in the near future.

Clearly this is the kind of an investigation that could be undertaken only by the government itself. It is the sort of an investigation, however, that is altogether necessary if the work now being done is to be made as nearly complete and accurate as possible. Despite the many inaccuracies that could scarcely be avoided in them, data gathered by this means would be invaluable as a check upon past estimates and as a basis for future work.

Returning to the sample statement given in the preceding pages, it is of course recognized that this identical arrangement of items would not serve for all countries. For example, some countries may have net outgo for merchandise, for emigrants' remittances, etc., instead of net income. If so, it is obvious that the position of these items in the income account would be changed. Such changes in detail, however, would not change the essential character of the several reports nor the interrelations between them—matters which have already been discussed at some length in Chapter V.

II. Some Questions of Definition

The fact that a balance sheet and a summary of current capital transactions are included in this sample statement of the international accounts, raises questions concerning the valuation of the items included. Here the statistician faces some of the most difficult—and likewise some of the most interesting—questions of accounting theory.

In the case of the income account of an ordinary business concern day-to-day record is kept of most of its component items. Purchases and sales, wage bills and interest payments, charges for heat, light, and rent, are matters of record, not of

estimate.[3] At the end of an accounting period, therefore, the accountant has in hand records covering the period that he is to summarize, and covering most of the items that will appear in this account. In drawing up the balance sheet, however, his problem is somewhat different.

The valuation of the assets of a business concern involves questions of judgment as well as matters of record. This is true both of physical assets, which are subject to wear and tear and obsolescence, and of assets represented by securities; while the valuation of intangibles, such as good-will, is almost altogether a matter of estimate.

A rule that has been generally adopted with regard to the initial valuation of all classes of assets is that they should be listed at their cost price, "even though the purchaser thinks he has bought at a great bargain." This seems a simple enough statement, but its interpretation is not always so simple a matter. In particular, it is sometimes very difficult to determine just what expenditures have entered into the cost of some specific asset. Many questions of this nature have been widely debated by accountants and economists, a goodly number have found their way into the courts for decision, and certain of them have also become the subject of statute law.

To illustrate, a corporation wishing to increase the capacity of its plant, issues bonds to secure the necessary funds for putting up a new building. During the time that the work is under way, interest on the bonds becomes due and is paid. The question is, should these interest payments be treated as part of the cost of the new building, or should they be charged as an expense against the income of the company? A similar question must be answered concerning the services rendered by the underwriters of the bonds. According to present practice in the United States, and by statute law in both Great Britain

[3] We are speaking here of total income or outgo on these accounts, and not of the problem of allocating expenditures to different departments of a business.

and Germany, the interest so paid is chargeable against "construction account," and thereby enters into the original cost of the new building. The cost of floating the loan is also considered as an item of cost and not as an expense.[4]

Once the original entry for an asset has been made, other questions arise in connection with its subsequent revaluations: Should the basis for revaluation be the initial cost price, the current market price, present value to the holder, or liquidation value? The theory that has come to be universally accepted is that for inventory or balance sheet purposes, assets should be listed at the value which they then have to their holder. But again practical questions of interpretation are involved. Without stating the various arguments upon which current usage is based, it may be said that in general the value of a particular asset to its holder is determined by the use for which it is intended. It is considered legitimate to hold at cost-price those assets which are acquired for permanent or long-continued use, even though there may have been a decline in their market value. But for those assets whose use is relatively short-lived, or which are purchased for resale as merchandise, it is a custom of long standing in America to fix the value at cost or market price, whichever is lower.[5]

Aside from current price fluctuations, practically all fixed assets—with the exception of land—suffer loss of value with the passage of time. For example, machinery and tools wear out with use; rust out with disuse; and regardless of use or disuse, become obsolete as new inventions take their place. Accounting theory and practice provide that deductions shall be made periodically from the value of such assets to allow for

[4] See Hatfield, H. R., *Accounting*, 1927, pp. 68-71; Esquerré, Paul-Joseph, *The Applied Theory of Accounts*, 1917, p. 33.

[5] Hatfield, *Accounting*, pp. 73-78, 99-109; Montgomery, R. H., *Auditing Theory and Practice*, 1917, pp. 552-556; see also his discussion in the revised edition, 1922, I, pp. 126, 145-146, and in *Auditing Principles*, p. 153. Esquerré disagrees with this view, p. 171.

losses of this type. The explanatory item, which is carried in the income account, is called "depreciation."

The application of these several rules to the valuation of assets in the form of securities raises some interesting problems concerning the question of initial and subsequent valuations. For example, a bond is bought at a discount, say at 93; in the course of time the market sags, so that by the end of the year the bond stands well below its purchase price; later there is a recovery, and by the end of the second year it exceeds the price at which it was originally purchased. A second bond is bought at a premium, say at 105; rises shortly after to 106, and thereafter shows a narrow range of fluctuation, with a general downward trend, until at maturity it stands at 100.

What is the value of these two bonds to their holder? If bought for speculative purposes, or as part of the "stock in trade" of the dealer, the general rules stated above would indicate that they should be entered at cost price—at 93 in the one case and at 105 in the other—and that in subsequent inventories and balance sheets they should be listed at cost or market price, whichever is lower.[6] On the other hand, if the bonds were bought as real investments, conformity with the general rules covering permanent investments would require that they should be kept on the books of the company at their original cost-price. As a matter of fact, there are differences of opinion and of law on this point. Austrian law, prior to the war, held that market-price should always be given—

[6] Esquerré argues against this, pp. 262-3, his argument here being in line with the position that he takes on the valuation of the inventory of any trading concern, p. 171. Montgomery, however, specifically says "the investments of a speculative finance company are its stock-in-trade and should be valued in the same way as stock on hand is valued in the case of mercantile undertakings, viz., 'cost or market, whichever is lower.'" (*Auditing Theory and Practice,* 1917, p. 555.) And in this connection, in his later edition of the same book, he says, "The rule (cost or market) is a good one and applies better than in the case of merchandise inventories." (1922, I, p. 111.)

whether this was higher or lower than original cost; and in the law passed June 4, 1925, this provision was again adopted. German law, on the other hand, holds for market or cost price, whichever is lower. This is also customary in Belgium, and is in process of becoming statute law in Czechoslovakia. In the United States, the practice of conservative accountants is on the whole in line with German law. The position taken by statute law and by the courts in the United States, and also in Great Britain, however, is in favor of disregarding market-price changes in securities which are held as permanent investment.[7]

In the case of bonds, accounting theory would further qualify the rule requiring that an asset bought for investment, and not for resale, should subsequently be listed at cost. If the two bonds discussed in the preceding paragraph were listed at cost-price at the time of their purchase, it is evident that at maturity the one bought at 93 would have a book valuation well below its redemption value, whereas the one bought at 105 would be over-valued. Such discrepancies, of course, would not appear in the case of bonds having no maturity date or having so long a duration that they are practically perpetual securities. But with a bond of ordinary length of life, selling above or below par, strict conformity with accounting theory requires that the difference between cost and par be gradually written off, for the theoretical explanation of the purpose of a premium or discount is that it is a means of adjusting the nominal rate of interest to the market rate for a given security. A premium represents a lump sum paid in advance to offset future interest payments at a rate above the market rate; whereas a discount represents an allowance of interest in advance, to compensate for future interest payments at something less than the market

[7] Hatfield, *Accounting*, pp. 88-89. For a fuller statement concerning Germany, Belgium, and Czechoslovakia, see an article by Léon Dupriez in the *Revue Economique Internationale*, February, 1927, pp. 248-250, and 258.

rate. As successive coupons come due and are paid, the holder of the bond receives interest plus or minus a sum which represents a capital adjustment. As the bonds approach maturity, therefore, their book value gradually approaches par.

This is the line of reasoning taken by accounting theory. Accounting practice and the decisions of the courts, however, are not entirely in agreement with theory on this point. It has been pretty generally argued that bonds bought at a premium should gradually be written down in value as they approach maturity, but many practical and legal objections are raised against writing up bonds bought at a discount.[8]

The valuation of investments represented by stock of other corporations is much less difficult. The stock certificate contains no promise that a certain sum of money will be repaid at a given time; and thus there is no problem of bringing book valuation into conformity with repayment value. So long as the stock is held as an investment, and so long as a change in market price is not realized through sale of the stock, the general rules concerning the valuation of securities will apply.

These many valuation questions, and some additional ones, face the statistician who compiles the international balance sheet. It has been pointed out in Chapter V that the international assets of a nation are the claims—both long-term and short-term—that it holds against foreigners. The long-term assets divide into security holdings (stock and bonds of foreign corporations, of foreign governments, etc.) and direct investments in foreign enterprises, foreign real estate, etc. Short-term assets consist of all commercial loans (credits extended on open account, promissory notes, bills discounted, etc.) of deposits in foreign banks, and of holdings of foreign currency notes. The question is, what rules should apply in the valuation of these several classes of assets.

So far as legal and accounting practice is concerned, there is no one answer that would be internationally acceptable. This

[8] Hatfield, *Accounting,* pp. 94-95: Esquerré, *The Applied Theory of Accounts,* pp. 227-34, 279.

conclusion follows when one considers the lack of uniformity that exists between the positions taken by various countries regarding the proper bases for investory and balance sheet valuations of assets. The International Institute of Statistics, many years ago, attempted to obviate this particular hindrance to the work it was doing. In 1901, in drawing up the program for the next meeting to be held two years later, the Institute asked its members to co-operate with Neymarck in considering, from the point of view of the work in international statistics, how the balance sheets of limited liability companies (des sociétés anonymes) could best be compiled and presented. At the meeting held in 1903, full reports were presented covering the laws and practices of various countries, but apparently nothing further was accomplished. Two years later de Foville referred to the difficulties involved in studies of international debts and investments through want of agreement concerning methods of valuing the items.[9] In 1927 the question still remains to vex us.

Even more troublesome than these theoretical questions are the practical difficulties involved in the collection of the data. Anticipating Chapter VIII, where available data are discussed, we may say that the balance-sheet information which the statistician is now able to secure falls far short of the precision attainable in accounting. Fair approximations, reasonable accuracy, compensating errors: these are necessarily the stock terms used in appraising available data concerning international movements of capital and concerning existing international obligations and claims of various countries.

Obviously, therefore, the niceties of method which the accountant adopts for dealing with discounts and premiums on securities, depreciation of physical assets, obsolescence of pat-

[9] *Bulletin de l'Institut international de Statistique,* Vol. XIV, 1903, Part 2, pp. 143-202; Vol. XV, Part 2, 1905, p. 199. Most of Paul Leroy-Beaulieu's criticisms of the French government's figures of French investments abroad in 1902 were concerned with this question of the valuation of the assets. (*L'Économiste Français,* October, 1902, pp. 449-451, 513-515, 549-555.

ents, losses from bad debts, etc., would be out of place in the hands of the international statistician. He must rely upon the "law of large numbers" or the "law of averages," testing his results by detailed information where such information is to be had.

At the stage now reached in the development of the international accounts, it would seem best to be governed by practical considerations in adopting methods of valuing the various classes of assets. But in the meantime, the theoretical discussions under way a quarter of a century ago might profitably be resumed by the statistician and the accountant. On the grounds of expediency, purchases and sales of bonds should be shown in the balance sheet at par, disregarding premiums and discounts.[10] This would do away with the necessity for later adjustments in values at maturity dates. But to make the statement of current capital transactions check with the income account the amount added into the total receipts or expenditures for bonds is exclusive of the discount item. (See page 97.)

For other classes of investments, the rules followed in business would probably give the best practical results, that is, initial valuations should be at cost price, as nearly as that can be ascertained. This valuation would be the one most nearly in harmony with valuations included in subsequent statements—where an attempt would be made at approximating the current value to holders. Particularly in the case of new issues of stocks, cost price, rather than par value, should be taken in recording transfers of new issues. After their original inclusion in the balance sheet, bonds would continue to be listed at par, other assets at a figure as nearly their current value as could be ascertained. Any nice distinctions here as to the proper basis for determining this current value would scarcely be feasible; for some classes of assets, market price

[10] Premiums and discounts would, however, be shown in the statement for current capital transactions—see sample statement.

alone would be available; and for others, only cost price. If both were to be had, the statistician would probably be governed in his choice by the laws and customs of his own country.

Referring back to the sample statement presented in Section I of this chapter, it will be seen that no allowance is made there for losses suffered during the course of the year from the depreciation of physical assets, from business failures with consequent loss in value of certain securities, from earthquakes, fires, and floods in regions where the investments of X had been placed, nor from any other possible cause. The explanation is that it probably would be unwise to undertake to collect data of this type annually. There is no doubt but that at the present time sentiment would be overwhelmingly against such a venture. In the long run, however, such losses total to enormous sums. It is partly for this reason that the proposal was made, in Section I, for a periodic census of foreign debts and investments as a basis for adjusting balance sheet data already available.[11]

Losses, whether from ordinary depreciation or from unusual causes, would by this method be carried directly to the balance sheet. It is not proposed that they should be shown in the income account, for in the case of the international accounts there is less reason than in business accounting for distinguishing sharply between the profit and loss items that may be carried directly to the balance sheet and those that must be carried through the income account. An explanation follows.

It is in the income account of the business concern that its *profits* from current operations are determined. If any unusual capital loss is included in the income statement for a given year, therefore, the result is to cut down the profits

[11] The official census of French investments abroad, taken in 1902—see discussion pp. 26-27—was severely criticized by Leroy-Beaulieu on the ground that many foreign assets were included at their original value despite the fact that some of them had become practically valueless.

shown for the year. If these losses are entered in the balance sheet, being shown there as a deduction from particular assets, the net worth of the business may be reduced, without a corresponding reduction being shown in operating profits—and consequently of dividends—for the year.[12]

But the international income account of a nation does not show *profits* from the year's operations. To do this it would be necessary to take account of all trade and production activities of the country, internal as well as external. The international income account can only show the net change in the international debts or investments, without indicating whether these came as a result of real earnings for the year or whether they came from the sacrifice of some national asset. With regard to the international accounts, therefore, it is immaterial from the point of view of legal and accounting theory, whether losses in the value of various assets be carried through the income account, or not. Accordingly, the decision may be made on the grounds of practical expediency.

If a census of foreign debts and investments is taken periodically, any necessary adjustments in the valuation of balance sheet items will probably best be determined by the results of this census. The revised balance sheet, in which the corrected data will then be presented, will require explanation. Some adjustments will have been made for the purpose of correcting accumulated errors. Others will have to take account of special losses such as are discussed on pages 65 and 107-108. Probably the clearest and easiest way of handling this explanatory material would be to append to the periodically corrected balance sheet a special report covering all of the adjustments that had been made.

[12] See Hatfield, H. R., *Accounting*, pp. 268-271. Here this question is thoroughly discussed from the business viewpoint, and a great many citations are given of legal opinion and legal decisions, both for and against requiring that special losses be carried through the income account.

CHAPTER VIII

THE DATA

However clear-cut may be the story told by a set of accounts, their value must depend primarily upon the approximate accuracy of the tale they tell. This reflection calls for some consideration of the data available for drawing up the international accounts. Are they reliable enough to warrant the adoption of the accountant's financial statement, with its appearance of completeness and accuracy? Is it worth while attempting to check one set of items against another, when the estimates for some of them represent little more than brave guesses?

This objection will probably be raised against the proposed inclusion of the balance sheet. It is the same criticism that is frequently leveled at the United States Department of Commerce—and at the League of Nations—for their attempts to get estimates for the various classes of current capital transactions. In fact, it is in this fashion that the skeptic sometimes takes to task all those who would attempt any study of the accounts, or would draw any conclusions from them.

I. Trade and Service Items

Anyone who has made a study of the question will readily admit that the estimates for some of the trade and service items in the income account represent little more than "discriminating deductions from current knowledge and impressions, which are usually somewhat indefinite and not always thoroughly reliable." For other items, fairly satisfactory records are to be had.

The largest items in the income account for any country are the official figures for commodity trade. In general, these are based upon documents filed with the customs authorities when the goods are brought into or taken out of the country in question. The information required by the customs officials varies, of course, from country to country; and there is also great diversity in the systems of compiling the data thus collected. Likewise, the official methods adopted for collecting and reporting the trade of a given country are likely to show some changes from one year to another. For example, the League of Nations reports that of the 46 countries for which both pre-war and post-war trade figures are available, only 16 have preserved complete comparability for either total imports or total exports, throughout the whole period 1910-1924.[1]

The user of trade data, therefore, must be on guard that his interpretation of the figures takes full account of possible divergencies—and possible inaccuracies—in method. In the main these pertain to the trade year employed, the territory covered by the data, the inclusiveness of the figures, methods of valuing the trade, and currency fluctuations. The question of the trade year is one which, as a rule, can be easily disposed of, however the figures are used. The other four points, however, require some explanation.[2]

1. The foreign trade of a country usually is thought of as the trade which it carries on with the outside world. But to

[1] *Memorandum on Balance of Payments and Foreign Trade Balances, 1910-1924,* Part II, p. 5.

[2] The discussion will be confined to those divergencies that affect the use of the trade figures in the international accounts of a single country for a single year. It will not deal with the question of year-to-year comparisons of the figures for a single country, nor with the validity of conclusions based upon comparing the import figures of one country, say, with the export figures of the countries from which such imports are said to have come. Neither will it take up differences in the classification of trade data, with the many questions that would be involved in such a discussion.

make this statement exact, it is necessary to define what is meant by the outside world. In particular, it is necessary to know how the outlying possessions of a country are classified. In the statistics for the United States, trade with the Philippine and Virgin Islands is considered foreign, these being the only outlying possessions of the United States having their own currency and banks of issue;[3] trade with other outlying possessions is considered domestic. Practically all other nations treat as foreign trade not only their commerce with foreign nations, but also that with their own outlying possessions.

This latter practice has been the subject of recent criticism by French financiers and economists who argue that, for France, the international accounts should include all international transactions that affect the value of the franc. They hold that to make the accounts adequate from the standpoint of the currency problem, the colonies using the French franc should be considered as part of France, while Indo-China, the one colony having a separate currency, should be treated as a foreign country. Thus they would follow the practice adopted by the United States. For certain purposes, however, it is preferable that the accounts for the mother country should not be confused with those for the colonies. It would seem, therefore, that for a country whose outlying possessions have no independent currency but do have a relatively important foreign trade, two sets of accounts are required: one of these should show the mother country as an independent unit, the other should give a consolidated statement for the mother country and these outlying possessions.[4]

[3] The political status of the Philippines is an additional reason for this differentiation; while in the case of the Virgin Islands the principal port is a free port—and in general the trade of a free port is recorded in the same way as "warehouse" trade.

[4] It should be noted that, whereas the statistical reports published by the United States give data covering the foreign trade of her outlying possessions, the colonies of France have their own statistical organizations, and put out their own trade reports. The fact that these colonial

2. For the purposes of the international accounts the foreign trade figures should show what goods a nation has purchased for home consumption, and what "national produce" it has exported to other countries. Offhand, this seems an obvious and simple statement, but it is sometimes no easy matter to appraise and adjust available data in the light of this requirement. Difficulties may arise from any one of a number of causes: from the system which government officials have adopted for compiling the data; the official exclusion from the records of certain types of imports and exports; clerical errors in the compilation of the data; or from evasions or carelessness on the part of the importer or exporter.

So far as official practices are concerned, these are usually explained at some length in the trade reports. For example, the careful worker may ascertain from the trade reports whether the figures given for imports are inclusive or exclusive of goods brought in for re-export, whether or not goods passing through the country in transit are included among the recorded imports and exports; how the movement of warehoused goods is recorded, etc. He will also find what exceptions are made from the general plan that has been adopted for collecting and compiling the data; for example, that British trade figures do not include the greater part of the diamonds and precious stones imported and exported; that parcels post goods are not recorded by some countries, and are by others; that sales and purchases of ships are variously handled, etc. Clerical errors are beyond his control, whether made by the merchant reporting a transaction, or by customs house officials. And smuggling, which succeeds only by escaping detection, can only be estimated in a very rough way.

3. The trade figures used in the international accounts should show the cost of imports and the receipts from exports. This

reports are often very late in making their appearance makes it very difficult to present currently the combined data for France and her colonies.

apparently is the theory accepted in all countries, but it is interpreted in a great many different ways in the practical collection and compilation of trade data.

One outstanding difference in practice arises over the question of how, or by whom, the trade should be valued. On this point, the systems of valuation adopted by different countries roughly divide into "official" and "declared." Official values are values fixed by government authority. Declared values, as the term implies, are values declared by importers and exporters at the time the goods pass customs, with whatever alterations are officially made by the authorities.

The explanation for this difference is largely historical. When the recording of trade data by the customs authorities first came into practice, merchants were required to report their imports and exports in quantity terms, these being subject to certain checks at the customs houses. The value of the trade, however, was roughly calculated from these quantity data and from current price information gathered by the government. Price data collected in this way being unsatisfactory, the next step taken in many cases was for the government to institute a price inquiry for the purpose of fixing a "permanent schedule" of values. Once established, this schedule was likely to remain in force for decades. For example, in Great Britain the schedule fixed in 1692 was still employed in the valuation of imports down to 1854. In France, the schedule drawn up in 1827 remained in use until 1847. This method was also unsatisfactory, for it did not take account of fluctuations in the prices of particular goods or changes in the general price level. To remedy this, the "permanent schedule" was discarded and a commission of experts was created whose function was to draw up a schedule of values to be used in valuing the trade, this schedule, as a rule, being subject to annual revision.

By a historical accident Great Britain changed the method used in valuing her exports from that of official values based on the old permanent schedule, to that of declared values. This

change came during the Napoleonic wars, as a result of a special charge which the government had levied upon exports to meet the expense of convoys provided to protect outgoing merchandise. Finding that the system of official valuations would not furnish an equitable basis for the assessment of this charge, the government required that exporters declare the actual value of their goods. No change was made in the method of valuing imports, however, and down to 1854, as we have said, these were still officially valued on the basis of the permanent schedule established in 1692. At that time a commission of experts was appointed to work out and periodically revise a schedule to be used in the valuation of imports. Finally, in 1871, the method of declared values was adopted for imports as well as for exports. Countries that are members of the British Empire all now follow the British practice in this respect.

In other countries the change from official values has come slowly, in most cases having been made during or since the World War. In fact, Hungary, Roumania, Argentina, Paraguay, Uruguay, Spain, and Peru have not yet broken away from the older method. Although France adopted declared values for imports in 1922, she still uses official values for exports; and Norway, having in the same year made the change for exports, still officially values her imports. War and post-war changes that have been made, have largely been necessitated by currency fluctuations, and by attendant difficulties in assessing and collecting customs duties.[5]

The opinion is pretty generally held that declared values are likely to be much more satisfactory for the purposes of the

[5] For a further discussion of British trade statistics see Giffen, Sir Robert, *Statistics;* for French statistics, Moulton and Lewis, *The French Debt Problem,* Appendix A; and for complete information concerning the trade statistics of all countries see the two volumes *Memorandum on Balance of Payments and Foreign Trade Balances,* published by the League of Nations.

international accounts than are official values. However, in countries where official practice requires that the declarer report, not the price involved in the purchase or sale of his goods, but a value defined for tariff purposes, certain errors may result. For example, in countries requiring that importers declare their goods on the basis of "fair market value for home consumption in the country of export," declared values will be higher than commercial values for goods brought from countries where export prices are below internal prices; and vice versa. And, as the League of Nations points out, a biased statistical error necessarily is involved in the import statistics of countries which provide that imports be based either on "invoice" values or "on consumption values in the country of export," whichever is higher—Canada, the Union of South Africa, and since May, 1921, the United States.[6]

A second difference in the methods used by various countries in valuing their trade arises over the question of when or where the value should be set. This difference in definition applies particularly to imports. Exports, without exception, are valued f. o. b. (free on board). That is, they are valued at the frontier of the exporting country, no allowance being made for insurance, shipping charges, and so on, beyond that point. Imports, on the other hand, are in a great many cases valued c. i. f. (cost, insurance, freight). If so, the value recorded is the value at the frontier of the importing country, and is inclusive of export duties, insurance, freight, commission charges, and so on, to that point, and as a rule is exclusive of import duties and other charges beyond the frontier of the importing country. This is the practice followed in Europe, and also in a great many other countries. The practice followed by a large number of countries in the American hemisphere, and by a few others, is to value imports, like exports, on an f. o. b. basis.

Both methods are variously defended and opposed. In a

[6] *Memorandum on Balance of Payments, 1910-1924,* Vol. II, p. 12.

Canadian inquiry the stand was firmly taken that the f. o. b. basis for valuing imports "is the better plan of the two because the values there given are accurate so far as they go."[7] The League of Nations, on the other hand, apparently approves of c. i. f. valuations, stating that "This is in accord with commercial practice, whether the freight is prepaid or collected on delivery."[8] Of the countries whose trade statistics are included in the League's *Memorandum,* approximately three-fourths have adopted the c. i. f. basis for import valuations.

4. Trade statistics in value terms are difficult to compile and to interpret for countries whose currencies show wide fluctuations. For such countries, paper currency data are likely to have little meaning, and it is also difficult to find a satisfactory basis upon which paper values may be converted into some stable unit of value. During the post-war period many countries have had to face this question. Some have attempted to convert from paper to gold values, using various methods of determining the conversion ration to be used.[9] Others have converted to 1913 values by applying a 1913 price schedule to classified data showing the post-war volume of trade, a method which does not take account of the change in the value of gold nor the shift in the relative price level of various classes of commodities. In whatever way the figures are reported for countries with an unstable currency, the use of value data should take account of possible errors involved in their compilation, and of their degree of comparability with other items in the international accounts.

Figures showing the movement of gold and silver are much less satisfactory than the commodity trade figures. Léon Say, in his study of the French indemnity of 1871, commented on

[7] *Minutes of Evidence,* August, 1915 (Cd. 7971), p. 167.

[8] *Memorandum on Balance of Payments, 1910-1924,* Vol. II, p. 13.

[9] See for example my discussion of the German trade figures during the time of the rapid depreciation of the mark, in Moulton and McGuire, *Germany's Capacity to Pay,* Appendix A, pp. 284-7.

"the inaccuracy in the customs statistics concerning gold, saying that "this had been discovered in various investigations with regard to banks and money."[10] His conclusions, based upon a study of the official figures for 1871-1873, were that these data gave a figure for net exports that was too low, particularly for gold. In 1887 the difficulties peculiar to the collection of import and export statistics for gold and silver were raised for discussion by the International Institute of Statistics. The opinion there expressed was that the official figures compiled from customs house records were too low, and should be supplemented by data required from shipping companies.[11] At the session held two years later, a special committee reporting on the comparability of commercial statistics recommended that banks and other credit institutions be asked for information to supplement data compiled by the customs houses.[12] At the present time, a few countries publish no reports concerning their trade in the precious metals—Albania, Russia, and Paraguay. Certain others give only partial statistics—Bulgaria, Esthonia, Greece, Latvia, and Roumania. This way out of the difficulty, however, can scarcely be recommended to others.

Errors and omissions involved in the compilation of bullion and specie data may be due to a number of causes. Gold carried in the pockets of travelers, as a rule, is not taken account of by the authorities. Gold shipments are of relatively small bulk and may at times be passed across the frontier without detection. And, as Sir Robert Giffen pointed out, it is probable that, in order to evade the higher freights that would otherwise have to be paid, gold is sometimes sent from one place to another under the description of silver.[13] On the whole, these errors are likely to be of minor importance,

[10] *Rapport sur le paiement de l'indemnité de guerre*, 1874, p. 62.
[11] *Bulletin de l'Institut international Statistique*, Vol. II, part I, p. 235.
[12] *ibid.*, Vol. IV, Part II, p. 275.
[13] *Statistics*, p. 86.

but during exceptional years a considerable error may be introduced into the international accounts if these figures are used without correction.

The shipping item in the accounts may be estimated in various ways. Giffen explored this subject pretty thoroughly in 1882. First he called attention to the fact that the import figures for all countries taken together total larger than exports, the difference representing the cost of shipping, insurance, commissions, etc. After making a deduction for insurance, commissions, etc., he proceeded to apportion the remainder—representing the total shipping earnings of the world—on the basis of the tonnage owned by each country. Shipping earnings thus determined for a country are then corrected to take account of the charges which the country's ships must pay in foreign harbors, and for the income which the country receives from foreign ships within its own harbors. This method, it will be seen, does not take account of the fact that many countries value their trade on an f. o. b. basis, their import figures thus being exclusive of insurance, freight, etc. This fact, however, was of much less relative importance at the time Giffen wrote than it is today.[14]

A second method developed by Giffen, and followed by later writers, is that of determining the net earnings per ton of steamers and sailing vessels, deductions having been made for outlays abroad and for earnings in the coastwise traffic of the country. The calculations made by Giffen in following this method were based on the accounts of Great Britain's principal joint stock shipping companies, supplemented by information furnished by shipping companies concerning the earnings and expenditures of particular vessels. By applying this net earnings figure to the total tonnage on the country's register, the total shipping earnings of a country are roughly ascertained.

[14] *Journal of the Royal Statistical Society,* June, 1882, pp. 207-21 and 259-70.

A method followed by C. K. Hobson in his *Export of Capital* is that of estimating the total income that the shipping companies of a country must have to meet their operating costs and pay interest and dividends on their investment. This method, like those above, gives the total shipping income of a country, whether on exports and therefore paid by foreigners, or on imports and paid by the people of the country in question.

In the case of countries whose imports are valued c. i. f. and whose exports are valued f. o. b., this total figure, with appropriate corrections for port charges paid and received, is the figure that should be entered in the income statement. It will be seen that for such a country the shipping charges for imports carried by *foreign* vessels have already been included in the value of imports and should not, therefore, be entered a second time as an "outgo" shipping item in the statement. Second, it will be seen that imports brought in by the vessels belonging to this country are included in the value of imports, notwithstanding the fact that these merely represent payments from one group of its nationals to another. And since imports have not cost the nation as much (by the amount of the import shipping charges paid to its own shipowner) as appears to be the case from the import figures, it is necessary that an adjustment be made in the account. This adjustment is made by including as part of the shipping earnings of the nation the part that it received from carrying imports for its own people.

Finally Giffen referred to a method which had already been used by other writers, and one which is still employed by the Department of Commerce in estimating the shipping income and outgo of the United States. Most countries keep a record of the value of their trade carried in ships of their own nationals or of foreigners. By determining the ratio that shipping charges, on the average, bear to imports and to exports, it is then easy to estimate the shipping earnings, and expenditures, of a country. For a country whose imports are valued

c. i. f., the import ratio is applied to all imports brought in by ships belonging to its own people—for reasons explained in the paragraph above. The export ratio is also applied to all exports carried away in the ships of its own people. For a country whose imports are valued f. o. b., the import ratio is applied to all imports brought in in foreign ships—this representing the outgo that its own people must pay for shipping. The export ratio is applied to all exports carried away in its own ships—this representing its income from shipping. In both cases, an amount must be added for the earnings of its ships engaged in carrying goods from one foreign country to another; and an adjustment must be made for the expenditures of its ships in foreign harbors, and for income from foreign ships in its own harbors.

It is impossible, by any of these methods, to determine exactly the shipping items in the account. But by checking the results obtained by one method against those obtained by another, and by checking the reports of one country against those of another, fairly satisfactory approximations may be had.[15]

Probably less information is available concerning the insurance, banking, and commissions item, than for any other. Sir Robert Giffen estimated British income from this source at 2½ per cent of the total trade of the country, and most British investigators since his time have followed his method. France and the Union of South Africa estimate this item at 2 per cent of the value of imports, this estimate, in the case of France, covering maritime insurance alone. A few countries

[15] A rough and ready calculation of the shipping earnings of Germany, France, and Italy has been made by the Institute of Economics as follows: (a) A percentage comparison was made of the tonnage shown on the national register, and on Lloyd's, for the country in question and Great Britain. (b) This percentage was applied to the careful estimates that have been made of British shipping earnings. It will be seen that, even though independent methods are used for estimating the earnings of various countries, this method is useful as a check.

have reported to the League of Nations that they are securing the co-operation of insurance companies and banks in arriving at their estimates, and it may be that a more reliable basis for estimating will be developed in the future. In the meantime it is comforting to note that the sums involved in this class of transactions amount to a relatively small total as compared with other items in the income account.

The accuracy of the interest and dividends item depends largely upon the accuracy with which balance sheet items are known. Government payments and receipts of interest are, of course, matters of record, and the amount involved may easily be ascertained. So far as other income from foreign investments is concerned, this, as a rule, "can only be estimated on the basis of known investments and average yields.[16] A few countries state in their reports to the League of Nations that their banks have furnished information concerning the total payments and receipts made through their agency on account of foreign investments and foreign obligations; and others indicate that their banks have compiled rough balance sheets from which they have estimated the interest and dividends item.

Income tax returns are useful as a check against these data, but will not, of themselves, tell the whole story. In commenting upon the inadequacy of the income tax returns given in the reports of the Inland Revenue Commission of Great Britain, Giffen pointed out that while certain classes of income from abroad were identified in these reports, other classes were not. With regard to the first of these he said, "One has only to go over a stock and share list, like that of the 'Investor's Manual,' jot down the capital of the foreign issues brought out in this country, and which are wholly or mainly held here, to perceive that there is something wrong." And with regard to foreign income not distinguished in the reports from domestic income, he said, "We have also to consider

[16] *U. S. Trade Information Bulletin* 399, p. 14.

that there is a large British capital invested abroad privately, through mercantile houses having dependent houses abroad, through insurance companies doing business abroad, through Anglo-colonial banks receiving deposits here and investing them abroad." He therefore turned to the *Investor's Monthly Manual* and to banking supplements of the *Economist* for data on which to make his estimate.[17]

Sir George Paish, whose estimates of British investments abroad now serve as a basis for the *Board of Trade Journal's* estimates, explained that in order to correct the deficiencies in data published by the income tax authorities, he had "examined the reports, balance-sheets, and income statements of several thousand companies; in fact . . . the reports of all British companies working abroad about which official information could be obtained.[18] From these, together with the income tax data, he was able to classify British foreign investments by their geographic distribution and by the purposes for which the capital had been used. His estimate of the amount of British capital placed in New Zealand is used today by that Dominion in estimating the investments of foreigners on which her people must pay interest and dividends. India's estimate for this item is also indirectly based upon Paish's "balance sheet" data, for the Indian estimate is calculated on the assumption that about 10 per cent of Britain's capital, as shown by the *Board of Trade Journal* estimate, and a very small amount of additional foreign capital, is invested in India.

Information concerning emigrants' remittances is usually secured from banks or postal authorities. Private banks furnished this information for Finland. The Italian estimate of receipts from this source is usually based upon post-office returns with regard to money orders, and upon data furnished by the Bank of Naples—through which about one-fourth to one-fifth of the total of such transactions pass. Sweden turns

[17] *Journal of the Royal Statistical Society*, March, 1878, pp. 8, 31.

[18] *ibid.*, January, 1911.

to her postal statistics to determine the remittances received from her emigrants to the United States. France and Germany keep official records of the foreign workers within their boundaries, and from these data estimate the amounts that are sent back home by these people—or the sums carried back by those "migratory workers" who come and go for seasonal employment. The United States bases its estimate on Census figures showing the number of foreigners in the country, and on a rough estimate of the average amount sent home by each.[19]

Admittedly, all of these estimates are rough. It is sometimes possible to cross-check the results published, however, and thereby get some measure of their reliability. For example, the figure published by the Department of Commerce of the United States was questioned recently, particularly the estimate of the amount which Italian immigrants had sent back to Italy. To answer this criticism, the authorities at Washington cabled to its foreign representatives, asking for their estimate on this item. To the satisfaction of the Department, the answering cable brought substantial confirmation of their original figure.

The tourist item in the accounts is not subject to precise measurement. Average expenditures per traveler can be only roughly estimated from a survey of the opinions and observations of private tourist agencies and of public officials. With regard to the number of travelers involved, information for some countries is perhaps a little more definite. For the United States, whose tourist expenditures abroad amount to an enormous total, the Bureau of Immigration keeps a record of the number of Americans leaving the country, and of the number of foreigners traveling here. France and Switzerland, whose receipts from this trade bulk very large in their international accounts, have national tourist offices whose principal

[19] A thorough pre-war study of immigrants' remittances was made by C. F. Speare, see the *North American Review,* January, 1908, pp. 106-116.

purpose is to promote the trade but which incidentally collect some data concerning the numbers of incoming and outgoing foreigners. Official count of foreign visitors is also taken in New Zealand. Finland secures data of this sort from her police records. Germany estimates the number of her tourist visitors from data furnished by the principal resorts of the country. A few countries—among them being the United Kingdom—assume that tourist income and outgo are approximately equal, and, therefore, need not be estimated.

A number of other items are included in the accounts of various countries. Hungary includes revenue from patents, and income and outgo from the cinema industry. Motion picture royalties are also included in the accounts of the United States. An additional item in the accounts of the United States represents the charitable and missionary expenditures of the country, data on this score being furnished the government by the leading organizations engaged in foreign missionary and relief work. Some countries include estimates of their diplomatic and consular receipts and expenditures, while others assume that there is no net figure, one way or the other, of any importance. For some countries, railway earnings from carrying goods in transit for their neighbors amount to a considerable total and therefore must be set forth in the income account.

II. Current Capital Transactions

Until the outbreak of the war, little had been done toward compiling information with regard to the various loan and investment transactions currently carried on between the government and people of a particular country and foreign governments and people. Considerable progress has now been made, however, toward securing some information of this sort for a limited number of countries. In this connection, much credit must be given to the United States Department of

Commerce for the pioneering it is engaged in, and for the degree of success it has thus far been able to achieve.

The data required for drawing up a statement of current capital transactions for a given country are of two types—first, data pertaining to government borrowing and lending transactions; second, those concerning private credit transactions. Information of the first sort is a matter of official record, and can easily be made available. Complete data of the second class, pertaining both to long-term and short-term operations, have thus far proved difficult to obtain.[20]

Transactions in listed securities make up a large share of the long-term private operations, and these are comparatively easy to estimate. International transactions in securities are, for the most part, handled by a limited number of important banks in each country. It is reasonable to suppose, therefore, that if these banks will co-operate fully with the government, fairly accurate statistics concerning these transactions may eventually be made available. This is the assumption upon which the United States Department of Commerce has proceeded. With regard to the results thus far reached, the opinion of the Department is that their data on new loans publicly issued are fairly accurate, and that they have also been able to secure fairly satisfactory information with regard to sales and purchases of outstanding securities.[21]

So far as other forms of long-term investments are concerned, the Department of Commerce attempts no estimate. Germany and Hungary report figures on international dealings in real estate. The German figures are "estimated on the basis of individual cases."[22] The Hungarian Government does not

[20] The questionnaire which the U. S. Department of Commerce uses for securing these data is presented in Appendix B, pp. 159-165, together with a short history of its development.

[21] *Trade Information Bulletin 399*, p. 17.

[22] League of Nations *Memorandum on Balance of Payments, 1911-1925*, Vol. I, p. 35.

state the basis for its estimate. A number of countries report estimates for other forms of long term investments, but the basis for these estimates is not shown in the League of Nations report.

By far the most difficult questions arise in connection with unfunded borrowing and lending transactions. The United States has turned to the questionnaire method for collecting information from a large number of banks concerning foreign bank balances in this country and the balances of Americans in foreign banks. Italian accounts presented in the League of Nations *Memorandum* also give data on bank balances, presumably collected through the agency of Italian banks.

Information concerning open credits on trade account has thus far proved by far the most difficult to obtain. The German government contents itself with the observation that the two sides of the account probably balance so far as these dealings are concerned. The United States Department of Commerce made "no attempt . . . to obtain reports from manufacturers and export houses" with regard to outstanding debts and advances of credit on open account, concluding that "it is yet practically impossible to obtain adequate data on international open accounts." [23] From the lack of information on this point in the accounts of other nations, it is apparent that they agree with this observation.

III. Existing Foreign Assets and Liabilities

As in the case of current capital transactions, the data required for making up the international balance sheet for a country may be divided into two general classes. The first of these is concerned with government debts owed to foreigners and claims which the government holds against foreigners; the second, with all other classes of outstanding foreign obligations and outstanding claims against foreigners.

Data concerning government debts and loans are, of course,

[23] *Trade Information Bulletin 399*, p. 26.

matters of official record. It should, therefore, be fairly easy to obtain accurate information concerning the status of such international assets and liabilities at a given time. And these data, if published in such a way as to show their geographic distribution, will aid greatly in the compilation of balance sheet data for other countries. Whether the contracts represented by this class of balance sheet items can be carried out is, of course, a matter involving questions of judgment rather than of record. Here the statistician compiling the international accounts is on an equal footing with the corporation accountant, for uncertainties always appear wherever the future is involved.

For information concerning all other foreign assets and liabilities, estimates must be relied upon. A great many sources of material and methods of investigation may be used in the collection of these data. These may be roughly summarized as follows: (1) Earlier investigations furnish some basic data. (2) The large investment and banking houses of a country are always in a position to give fairly comprehensive data concerning the investments in foreign securities, or vice versa, concerning the foreign borrowings of their clients. (3) Associations of the holders of foreign bonds organized in several countries, gather a wealth of information concerning the outstanding foreign investments of their people. (4) Foreign consular and diplomatic agents of the government have at times been required by their governments to make surveys of the investments that their fellow-countrymen have made in the districts where they are located. (5) A survey of information currently published in the financial pages of newspapers and journals gives a valuable check upon other sources of information. (6) The annual compilation of an international income account showing the surplus available each year for new investments abroad—or the deficit met by new borrowings—indicates the growth in the net total of investments or debts, and furnishes an important check upon other methods of estimating the items entering into the balance sheet.

All of these methods have been applied in collecting data on foreign investments and foreign obligations represented by securities or by proprietary rights in trade and commercial enterprises and real estate. And while it is admitted that the data thus brought together are not, and cannot be, "absolutely accurate," nevertheless in many cases the investigations have been so carefully made that the resulting data are generally accepted as fair approximations of the actual situation. For example, the *Board of Trade Journal* in commenting upon Paish's data concerning Britain's foreign investments, says "Although there has been a good deal of criticism of the details of his calculations, there is substantial agreement among financial authorities in regard to the accuracy of the totals." [24]

It is with the collection of information concerning the short term, or floating, debts and investments that less experience has thus far been had. In the summary balance sheet published each year by the Statistical Department of the Danish government, the total set down for floating debts and floating credits of various classes is "obtained from a number of public authorities, financial institutions, commercial companies, and private business men." Information that we have, however, does not show how satisfactory were the returns thus obtained, nor how inclusive were the data presented.

The Department of Commerce of the United States has collected data concerning bank balances. Until recently, however, it had attempted nothing further concerning the short-term items in the balance sheet; although the study covering the year 1926 will deal with the question of short-term transactions in considerable detail. Questionnaires addressed to bankers on the subject of foreign balances have brought in a very large percentage of replies, but greater completeness is desirable in these data.[25]

A comparatively small, but for some purposes important,

[24] *Board of Trade Journal,* January, 1920, pp. 71-73.

[25] *Trade Information Bulletin 399,* p. 26.

class of assets and liabilities is represented by the open accounts of importers and exporters. Thus far data for these items have not been compiled by any country. Opinions have been expressed in numerical form, however. For example, Décamps took account of this item in his studies of the accounts of France, giving a rough estimate of the amounts involved.

Apparently at the present time the only way in which a complete total for the floating debts and investments, respectively, may be obtained, is by the use of the income accounts, supplemented by all available data from whatever source they may be had. From a long series of such studies it should be possible eventually to get fairly good data.

To summarize: The reliability of the data available for calculating or estimating the items in the international accounts varies greatly from country to country and from item to item. It is comforting to note that in all countries the largest items in the income account, commodity import and export data, are likewise the most reliable. Giffen estimated that in the case of Great Britain the error in these figures probably would not exceed 1 per cent one way or the other. The least reliable item of income or outgo, that with regard to insurance, commissions, etc., is the smallest. The accuracy of the interest item in the income account depends largely upon the accuracy of the balance sheet data available. In the statement of current capital transactions and in the balance sheet, the largest item is again the most reliable. The smallest items in these accounts are the ones concerning which it is most difficult to secure precise information, but they are also the ones that in normal times are likely to show least variation.

CHAPTER IX

IS THE PLAN PRACTICABLE?

The international accounts of a country, if they are to serve satisfactorily all the purposes for which they may be required, must include (1) the international income account for the period under consideration, (2) a statement of current capital transactions, and (3) a comparative international balance sheet showing the debt and investment position of the country at the beginning and end of the period. Compiled and presented in this way, they are easily interpreted by the reader, and they also furnish a means of checking one class of data against another that is very useful to the compiler of the accounts. Net income or net outgo shown by the income account must tally with the net results shown by the statement of current capital transactions, while the data presented in the statement of current capital transactions and in the initial balance sheet furnish the information needed for the compilation of the closing balance sheet.

To avoid cumulative errors in the balance sheet, one more requirement must be met. A periodic census of the foreign debts and foreign investments of the country should be taken, say, at five or ten year intervals. This would furnish an additional check upon the accounts presented in the "intercensal" years. Taken all in all, the task of compiling the accounts is so great that it is likely to be well done and regularly done only if it is handled by some arm of the government. These, in short, are the conclusions reached in the analysis presented in preceding chapters.

The practicability of this plan remains to be considered.

Against it there are certain to be some who will argue the inadequacy of available data. They will perhaps question the value of checking one class of data against another, when neither is entirely accurate and complete. They will probably argue the futility of attempting to compile an adjusted balance sheet each year on the basis of available data regarding current capital transactions. They will certainly point out the difficulties likely to be involved in a periodic census of foreign debts and investments, and the inaccuracies likely to be found in the results. And finally, some will doubtless object that if the work is to be done by a governmental agency, it will probably be handled in a routine and summary fashion, with errors cumulating and some pertinent data overlooked.

Admittedly, there is much truth in these objections. The difficulty is, however, to find an alternative plan that would be preferable. Possibly there are a few skeptics who would question the advisability of any continued work in this field unless and until the basic data are made thoroughly complete and reliable. But if pressed, these would be forced to admit the practical impossibility of ever getting absolutely complete and accurate data for all of the items included in the accounts.[1] The alternatives to some such plan as that proposed seem, therefore, to be as follows: either to continue the work as it is handled at present—see Chapter VI for examples and dis-

[1] Such a standard would, of course, be far beyond that which the accountant may hope to reach. Hatfield, for example, says: "Nor is it true that any set of books ever devised shows with perfect accuracy the state of the business even with the addition of a merchandise inventory. Inventories, at best, are approximate . . . Nor is it possible always to determine the exact nature of a business transaction so as to secure its correct entry in the books of account . . . the fact that in railroad accounting, where the system is the most elaborated of any business enterprise, the directors, from time to time, make correcting entries of enormous sums, implies that either before or after the correction the accounts were in essence incorrect, and that the system in reality broke down." *Modern Accounting*, 1913, pp. 31-32.

cussion of present-day methods—or to drop the whole task as a hopeless undertaking.

So far as the first of these is concerned, it would be difficult indeed to find anyone thoroughly satisfied with the reports now being published for any country. Those in charge of the work are as a rule the first to acknowledge its defects and to welcome suggestions for improvement. The second proposal is even less likely to be generally acceptable. Those most vehement in their criticisms of data now available would probably be even more vehement in their objection to a proposal for dropping all such investigations unless and until perfection might be reached. The whole tenor of our times is in favor of extending, rather than of narrowing, the limits of statistical inquiries. For example, the criticisms which British financial writers are leveling at the accounts now being published by the *Board of Trade Journal* have already been referred to in Chapter VI. But these critics, despite the fact that many of them seriously question the reliability of the data and of the findings published, are generally in favor of extending the scope of such investigations rather than of dropping the work. The following quotation from the *Manchester Guardian Commercial* will illustrate the point:

> In drawing attention to the nature of the evidence upon which the "Board of Trade Journal" writer has based his calculations of the "invisible exports" we are far from quarrelling with his results. He has done the best he could with the available material, and that the material is so deficient that no one with any pretence to scientific training can place any real faith in conclusions drawn from it is not his fault. But what is the moral? Surely that the subject is one which is crying out for systematic investigation. Such investigation must, no doubt, take the form largely of unofficial inquiry. It must be undertaken on an extended scale if valuable results are to follow. Is there not one among our economic organizations which is able and willing to undertake such a task? After all it is a matter of something more than academic interest to know

whether as a nation we are living within our means or whether we are falling into the debt of the external world.[2]

That satisfactory basic data are not available for estimating all of the items in the accounts goes without saying. This question has been discussed at some length in Chapter VIII. Improvement in these data is a probable future development, but even so, absolute accuracy is, in the nature of things, not to be expected. This being the case, the need for finding ways of checking and cross-checking the estimates entering into the accounts seems even greater than would otherwise be the case. The inadequacy of the data argues for, rather than against, setting up the accounts in such a way that each of the several reports may be easily and clearly interpreted and that its figures for net results may be compared with those shown by the other reports.

Once the statement of current capital transactions has been compiled and checked, it would seem to follow without question that its results should then be closed into the balance sheet. As we have said, there are some who will object that the data are too inaccurate to be used in this way. But if this objection is admitted, what value can be attached to the results presented in such a statement? Why should data be collected —as they now are—concerning capital movements?

For example, if the data compiled for a given year show that a country has incurred a certain net amount of new foreign obligations, this may be an interesting bit of information. To appreciate its full meaning, however, the reader must know whether or not in the past this country was a borrower or lender. And to appreciate the relative importance of the year's increase in foreign liabilities he must also know what the country's debt and investment position was at the beginning of the period. In short, he must have an initial balance sheet. If such a balance sheet is not compiled—and if such comparisons

[2] *Manchester Guardian Commercial,* February 5, 1925, p. 136.

are therefore made impossible—is it worth while bringing together the data on current capital transactions?

Inaccuracies in available data concerning current capital transactions will of course be reflected in the balance sheet in which such data have been incorporated. It is to meet this situation that the proposal has been made for a periodic census of foreign obligations and foreign investments. And even so, it must be admitted that absolutely accurate data cannot be hoped for—regardless of the method by which such a census is taken.

But the alternatives to making use of this and other checks that have been suggested do not, as we have said, offer a more nearly saitsfactory solution. To continue the work as it is being handled today, wtihout any attempt at a carefully compiled balance sheet, will not serve. It will mean that the interest and dividends item in the income account is almost certain to become more and more a hypothetical figure, and that the interpretation of the whole set of accounts will become more and more an uncertainty. On the other hand, there are few who would counsel the alternative suggestion—that work on the accounts be abandoned.

Finally, consideration must be given to the objection that satisfactory results are not likely to be attained if the task is taken over by an arm of the government. This objection, it may be said, is more likely to come from British and European writers than from Americans. For example, in the quotation from the *Manchester Guardian Commercial,* given on page 132, a plea is made for an "unofficial" inquiry.

As we have pointed out, the task of compiling the accounts is an enormous one. And if consecutive and comparable data are to be had, it is a never-ending task, for the data must be collected and presented year after year. Some very important single studies have been made in the past by "unofficial" investigators, but there are great gaps in our information concerning most countries. These have come as a result of the

fact that there was no one group officially responsible for the work. Furthermore, the government is in many cases in a better position to secure the co-operation of banks and business men generally than is the private investigator. Altogether, it would seem reasonable to expect a very substantial improvement in the reliability and completeness of the accounts if they are everywhere included within the province of the government statistician. And particularly is this the case if the several suggested methods of checking and cross-checking the data are adopted.

APPENDIX A

FORM AND CONTENT OF EARLIER STUDIES ILLUSTRATED

In Chapters II to V numerous references have been made to limitations in the form and content of earlier studies of the international accounts. Except for the length of most of these statements, it probably would have been desirable to have illustrated the points raised by presenting sample statements in the text or in the appended footnotes. That not being feasible, a limited number of such statements are brought together to form the present appendix. In choosing these samples, we have attempted to find compactly presented cases illustrating points raised in the discussion. We have, therefore, limited our choice to studies which present their summary conclusions in tabular or account form.

I. United States Census of Foreign Debts

The census of the foreign debts of the people of the United States, taken by the United States Treasury in 1853 in compliance with a resolution offered by Senator Brodhead and adopted by the Senate, furnishes a good example of a thorough piece of work which was limited in scope to a study of balance sheet data, and to only one large class of items that appear in the balance sheet.[1] The report of the Secretary of the Treasury presenting the results of this inquiry is given below. Ten statistical tables were appended to this report, the contents of which are described in the report. These descriptions indicate

[1] See discussion of this report in Chapter II, pp. 16-18.

the methods used in collecting the data and, together with the summary table, they also suffice to show the scope and the results of the inquiry.

REPORT OF THE SECRETARY OF THE TREASURY*

in answer
To a resolution of the Senate calling for the amount of American securities held in Europe and other foreign countries, on the 30th June, 1853.

March 2, 1854.—Ordered to lie on the table and be printed.

Treasury Department,
March 2, 1854.

Sir: The following resolution was adopted by the Senate on the 4th of April, 1853:

Resolved, That the Secretary of the Treasury be requested to procure, so far as practicable, and furnish the same to the Senate at the commencement of the next session of Congress, the following information, viz:

"The aggregate amount of federal, state, city, county, railroad, canal, and other corporation bonds, stocks, or other evidences of debt, held in Europe or other foreign countries, on the 30th of June, 1853, specifying separately, so far as the same can be ascertained, the amount of each of the above descriptions of bonds and stocks."

In compliance with the above resolution, I have the honor to submit the accompanying documents:

A.—A letter from the Register of the Treasury, dated February 27, 1854, giving the amount of federal stock outstanding on the 30th of June, 1853, and the amount estimated as then held by foreigners residing beyond the bounds of the United States.

B.—A general statement of the amount of bonds of the several States, outstanding on the 30th of June, 1853, and of the amount

* Senate Executive Document No. 42, 33d Congress, 1st Session.

thereof held by foreigners residing beyond the bounds of the United States, as well as could be ascertained, according to returns received at the Treasury Department from the chief officers of the different States.

C.—A table showing the amount of State bonds outstanding June 30, 1853, the amount of the same then held by foreigners residing beyond the bounds of the United States, according to the estimates of Winslow, Lanier, and Co., in the States marked with an asterisk, the amount of property held by various State governments, exclusive of school funds, according to the American Almanac for 1854, and the amount of real and personal estate subject to taxation in each State, according to the United States census returns for 1850.

D.—A statement of the amount of bonds of cities, towns, and counties, outstanding on the 30th of June, 1853, and of the amount thereof then held by foreigners residing beyond the limits of the United States, as far as could be ascertained, according to returns made to the Treasury Department, by the following cities, towns, and counties, and including some reported by brokers.

E.—A general statement of so many of the banks as have made returns of the amount of capital paid in, and the amount thereof held by foreigners on the 30th June, 1853.

F.—A general statement of so many insurance companies as have made returns to the Treasury Department.

G.—A general statement of so many railroad companies as have made returns to the Treasury Department, of the amount of capital authorized, the amount paid in, and the amount thereof held by foreigners, and also of the amount of bonds outstanding, and the amount thereof held by foreigners, so well as could be ascertained, on or near June 30, 1853.

H.—A general statement of so many canal and navigation companies as have made returns to the Treasury Department of the amount of capital authorized, the amount paid in, and the amount thereof held by foreigners, and also of the amount of bonds outstanding, and the amount thereof held by foreigners, June 30, 1853.

I.—A general statement of so many miscellaneous companies as have made returns to the Treasury Department of the amount of their capital authorized, the amount paid in, and the amount thereof

held by foreigners, and also of the amount of bonds outstanding, and the amount thereof held by foreigners, on the 30th June, 1853.

K.—A general summary of the foregoing documents.

It will be seen by reference to table K, taking Winslow, Lanier and Co.'s estimate as the criterion, that in June, 1853, the aggregate stocks and securities of the character set out in the table, held abroad, was $222,225,315.

The application of capital to railroads, commenced in 1829, and to canals, prior to that date, but we have no data from which we can state the amount of foreign indebtedness on those accounts. In 1829, the outstanding United States debt was about $58,400,000; a considerable part of which was then held abroad, and we know that a large amount of United States and other bank stocks was also held abroad, and it might be fair to estimate that the indebtedness of the same character as in the table K was as great in 1829 as it was in 1853, and that the annual interest and dividends to foreign holders of stocks and bonds has reached, for the last twenty-four years, about $13,000,000.

There is no data from which to make an aggregate statement of the capital that had been applied to canals, railroads, and the establishment of banks, insurance companies, etc., prior to 1829, and which, in connexion with table K, would exhibit the amount applied to those objects since; nor is there any data from which to estimate the value which the application of capital to canals, railroads, and banks, has given to the solid wealth of the country. All which is respectfully submitted.

Yours obedient servant,

JAMES GUTHRIE,
Secretary of the Treasury.

Hon. D. R. Atchison,
President pro tem of the Senate

As the report indicates, Table K briefly summarizes the data presented in the other nine tables appended to the report. It also shows the wide co-operation which the Treasury was able to secure from state, city, and county officials, and from large transportation, insurance, and other business concerns. Of the nine tables, therefore, Table K alone is reproduced here.

K

General Summary, June 30, 1853

	Total	Held by foreigners
United States stocks	$ 58,205,517	$ 27,000,000
State stocks (bonds)	190,718,221	72,931,507
113 cities and towns (bonds)	79,352,149	16,462,322
347 counties (bonds)	13,928,369	5,000,000
985 banks (stocks)	266,724,955	6,688,996
75 insurance companies (stocks)	12,829,730	378,172
244 railroad companies (stocks)	309,893,967	8,244,025
Do do (bonds)	170,111,552	43,888,752
16 canal and navigation companies (stocks)	35,888,918	554,900
Do do (bonds)	22,130,569	1,967,547
15 miscellaneous companies (stocks)	16,425,612	802,720
Do do (bonds)	2,358,323	265,773
Total	$1,178,567,882	$184,184,714

If the estimate of Winslow, Lanier and Co. be preferred, as to the amount of state stocks held by foreigners, $110,972,108 must be substituted in the second line of the second column, and the total will then be—

Aggregate of stocks and bonds	$1,178,567,882
Aggregate held by foreigners	222,225,315

At the time the resolution was voted requiring the debt inquiry to be made, Senator Brodhead presented to the Senate a rough estimate of the current income and outgo of the United States for the fiscal year 1851-52.[2] The statement presented by Brodhead is reproduced on page 141. It will be seen that it represents an income account used as a basis for estimating the year's foreign borrowings. The closing statement in the table clearly indicates that Brodhead recognized the relationship existing between the "income account" which he was presenting and the balance sheet data which he was urging should be collected. But since the results of the debt investigation were brought together about a year and a half after the presentation of this income account, the two can scarcely be said to represent a complete "financial statement."

[2] See discussion of this income account in Chapter II, pp. 16-17.

BRODHEAD'S INCOME ACCOUNT FOR THE UNITED STATES *

The amount current, then, of the United States for the last fiscal year with foreign countries will stand as follows:

Excess of imports over the exports of the country	$40,000,000
Interest annually payable to foreigners on the stocks, etc., held by them	18,000,000
Expenditures of travelers	5,000,000
Navy and diplomacy	3,000,000
Installment to Mexico	3,000,000
Remittances to Ireland	5,000,000
Total	$74,000,000
From this deduct the probable amount of gold and silver brought into the country by immigrants	10,000,000
Leaving the sum of	$64,000,000

as the balance against the United States, toward the settlement of which we have the official record of the exportation above the importations of $37,000,000 of gold and silver and the balance of $27,000,000 has no doubt been liquidated by the remittance of Federal, State, and other stocks.

* Appendix to the *Congressional Globe,* 32d Congress, 3d Session, 1853, p. 311.

II. French "Census" of Foreign Investments

The official inquiry of the French government, published in 1902, concerning the foreign investments of the French people, furnishes an example of a study limited in scope to one large class of assets in the international balance sheet. As published by the French government,[3] this report covers 32 large pages. A statement by John A. P. Mackenzie, published shortly afterward in the *Journal of the Royal Statistical Society* summarizes these data in a much more compact form, and at the same time clearly indicates the detail with which the information is presented in the official report. This summary follows on page 142.

[3] *Bulletin de statistique et de legislation comparée,* October, 1902, pp. 450-483. See discussion pp. 26-27 of this book.

MACKENZIE'S SUMMARY OF THE FRENCH INVESTIGATION OF 1902 *

Table showing in Million £ the Estimated Amounts of French Capital Invested in Different Countries, and the Principal Concerns in Which Those Investments Are Made.

Country	Commercial Houses	Lands	Banking and Assurance	Railways	Mining and Other Industries	Shipping, Harbours, etc.	State and Municipal Loans, etc.	Other Investments	Total
EUROPE	£	£	£	£	£	£	£	£	£
Russia	1.96	0.68	0.72	—	31.68	—	243.60	—	278.64
Spain	3.36	2.56	1.36	66.48	9.76	1.84	33.60	—	118.96
Austria-Hungary	—	0.12	—	80.00	1.96	—	31.60	0.32	114.00
Turkey in Europe	0.68	0.48	2.60	6.36	1.12	1.24	60.00	0.24	72.72
Italy	2.72	4.20	3.20	—	5.80	—	40.00	1.28	57.20
United Kingdom	0.60 [a]	—	—	—	0.12	—	36.00	3.28	40.00
Portugal	0.48	0.12	0.28	—	2.44	1.20	29.10	2.38	36.00
Belgium	—	12.00	—	3.20	2.40	—	4.00	2.40	24.00
Roumania ...	0.28	0.20	2.84	—	1.08	—	13.12	—	17.52
Switzerland ..	2.08	2.68	—	4.00	1.32	—	8.00	0.12	18.20
Norway	—	—	—	—	—	—	8.40	3.20	11.60
Greece	0.04	0.12	—	—	1.36	2.40	7.40	—	11.32
Servia	—	—	—	—	—	—	8.00	0.04	8.04
Holland	0.12	0.04	—	—	0.32	—	6.08	1.44	8.00
Monaco	0.76	1.04	0.52	—	—	—	4.00 [b]	—	6.32
Denmark	0.20	—	—	—	—	—	4.40	0.64	5.24
Sweden	—	—	—	—	—	—	4.92	—	4.92
Other countries	0.80	0.48	0.84	1.20	1.28	0.16	2.68	0.36	7.80
Total for Europe	14.08	24.72	12.36	161.24	60.64	6.84	544.90	15.70	840.48
ASIA									
China	2.40	1.88	—	—	0.20	—	21.56	—	26.04
Turkey in Asia	1.20	2.16	0.32	8.08	1.60	0.80	—	—	14.16
Other countries	0.65	1.17	—	—	1.28	—	—	1.54	4.64
Total for Asia	4.25	5.21	0.32	8.08	3.08	0.80	21.56	1.54	44.84
AFRICA									
Transvaal ...	0.20	0.20	—	—	60.00	—	—	2.16	62.56
Egypt	0.40	1.76	0.68	—	6.60	—	48.00	—	57.44
Tunis	4.12	4.64	0.88	2.40	0.48	—	7.96	—	20.48
Other countries	—	—	—	—	—	—	—	7.24	7.24
Total for Africa	4.72	6.60	1.56	2.40	67.08	—	55.96	9.40	147.72

MACKENZIE'S SUMMARY—(*Continued*)

Country	Commercial Houses	Lands	Banking and Assurance	Railways	Mining and Other Industries	Shipping, Harbors, etc.	State and Municipal Loans, etc.	Other Investments	Total
AMERICA	£	£	£	£	£	£	£	£	£
Argentina ...	—	14.64	2.12	4.0	1.28	—	12.40	2.48	36.92
Brazil	3.44	1.20	0.44	1.60	1.04	—	19.60	0.52	27.84
United States.	3.20	9.20	2.68	3.60	2.92	—	2.00	0.40	24.00
Mexico	2.00	4.00	0.80	—	3.20	—	—	2.00	12.00
Columbia	0.32	0.40	0.88	—	0.24	8.00	—	—	9.84
Chili	3.24	3.20	—	—	2.16	—	0.32	0.12	9.04
Uruguay	0.76[c]	5.52[c]	0.32[c]	—	0.56[c]	2.80[c]	1.92[c]	—	8.76
Canada	—	—	—	—	—	—	—	5.52	5.52
Venezuela ...	0.28	1.60	0.28	0.72	0.04	—	1.20	1.08	5.20
Cuba	0.04	4.00	—	—	1.00	—	—	—	5.04
Peru	1.00	2.40	—	—	0.76	—	0.08	0.04	4.28
Other countries	1.64	4.24	0.28	0.12	0.44	—	2.20	1.52	10.44
Total for America ...	15.92	50.40	7.80	10.04	13.64	10.80	39.72	13.68	158.88
OCEANIA									
Philippines ..	0.20	0.04	—	—	0.80	—	—	—	1.04
Other countries	0.64	0.36	—	—	—	—	—	0.24	1.24
Total for Oceania ...	0.84	0.40	—	—	0.80	—	—	0.24	2.28
Total ...	39.81	87.33	22.04	181.76	145.24	18.44	662.14	40.56	1,194.20

* *Journal of the Royal Statistical Society,* December, 1903, pp. 730-731.

[a] London only.

[b] Société des bains.

[c] These figures include both capital invested and the yearly gain therefrom.

The questionnaire used in securing this information from French diplomatic and consular representatives abroad was as follows:[4]

Are there in your district:

1. Any French commercial houses?

What is their form of organization?

[4] *Bulletin de statistique et de legislation comparée,* October, 1902, pp. 450-451.

At what figure would you estimate their fixed investment?
Principal branch of trade in which engaged.
Do they trade principally with France and the countries where they are located?
Do they have any important dealings with other countries, and any commission trade?

2. French-owned real estate?
Its value?

3. French-owned agricultural enterprises?
Their character? Their size? Their income?

4. French credits extended to any commercial, industrial, or agricultural enterprises?
In what form have they been extended?
Are they with or without guaranty?

5. French banks:
Their field of operation?

6. Ships under the French flag engaged in coastwise traffic?

7. French capital invested in ocean or river transportation companies?

8. French capital invested in railways?
Its yield?

9. French capital invested in mines and quarries?
Nature of these enterprises?
Estimate of the capital thus invested?
Evaluation of the yield of such capital?

10. French capital invested in industries?
What industries?
Estimated amount of these investments Their yield?

11. French holdings of agricultural land?
Their management? Are they exploited by the French owners?

12. Are there any other French-owned properties belonging to people living in your district, or any belonging to French people living in France or in other countries?
Their character? Their size? Their yield?

III. Debt and Income Accounts of the United States

One of the most thorough of the early studies of the international accounts of any country is that for the United States

made in 1869 by David A. Wells, Special Commissioner of the Revenue.[5] It contains a complete, careful and detailed statement of all classes of foreign liabilities of the people of the United States, including not only foreign-owned securities of the state and national governments, of railway and mining enterprises, and of other types of industry, but also bank loans, bills of exchange, real estate mortgages, etc. An accompanying income statement was presented by Wells to show the means by which this foreign indebtedness of the people was steadily increasing. Had a study of this sort been made annually, it would have answered practically all the purposes for which the accounts are required. As it was, however, many years passed before roughly comparable data were collected for the country.

EXCERPT FROM WELLS' REPORT *

At the breaking out of the war, in 1861, the distrust felt by nearly all foreigners in the future of the United States was so great that the larger portion of American securities—national, State, and corporate—held in foreign countries, were returned for sale at almost any sacrifice; and to such an extent was this the case that the country in 1863 may be said to have exhibited a clean national ledger in respect to foreign indebtedness. Since this date there have been transferred from the United States to foreign countries obligations which have raised the total of foreign indebtedness to an estimated amount of about $1,400,000,000, which may be classified somewhat as follows:

National Securities

In regard to the amount of national securities which have been transferred to *foreign* ownership since 1862-'3, the Commissioner finds a wide difference of opinion among American and European bankers best capable from experience of forming an estimate; the

[5] See discussion of this study, Chapter II, pp. 18-19.

* House of Representatives Executive Document, No. 27, 41st Congress, 2d Session (December 20, 1869) pp. XXVI-XXXI.

minimum being, however, from *seven* to *eight hundred millions.* The following estimate, prepared for the Commissioner by the house of Jay Cooke and Co., has not only received the approval of some of the largest purchasers of national securities on foreign account in New York, but has also been checked from various other and independent sources:

Fives of 1871 and 1874	$ 15,000,000
Sixes of 1881	90,000,000
Five-twenties of 1862	380,000,000
Five-twenties of 1864	30,000,000
Five-twenties of 1865, May and November	120,000,000
Five-twenties of 1865, January and July	200,000,000
Five-twenties of 1867	120,000,000
Ten-forties	25,000,000
Registered bonds of all issues	20,000,000
Total	$1,000,000,000

As substantiating the accuracy of the above estimate, it is to be noted that the earlier issues of United States securities have almost entirely disappeared from the American market, and that transactions are now limited mainly to the issues of July, 1865, 1867, and 1868.

Other Securities

State.—Of State securities held abroad or on *foreign* account the investigations of the Commissioner indicate a sum in excess of *one hundred millions.* The following amounts are returned as positively known to the State authorities:

Alabama	$ 1,483,260
Georgia	72,000
Illinois	1,400,000
Louisiana	5,235,933
Massachusetts	12,277,500
Michigan	800,000
Missouri	1,500,000
New York	2,440,999
Ohio	3,500,000
Pennsylvania	9,458,600
Virginia	7,523,500
Total	45,691,792

This amount, it is to be noted, only includes those issues which have been "placed" abroad originally through distinct State agencies. To it must be added the larger amount which has been from year to year purchased in the American market, and either sent abroad or held here on foreign account.

Railway bonds and shares.—Of railway bonds and shares held abroad or on foreign account, the investigations of the Commissioner indicate a total of $130,000,000 of bonds and $113,000,000 of shares.

Of the amount of bonds specified, an aggregate of $61,350,349 has been positively reported to the Commissioner in behalf of fourteen companies.

Of the amount of railway stocks specified, seven companies return an aggregate of $83,449,800. A detailed statement of this element of our foreign indebtedness would be given had not the information been communicated under a pledge that the details should not be made public.

For the companies which have not reported the amount of their stocks and bonds held abroad, estimates have been carefully prepared for the Commissioner by the best authorities on this subject. The character of these statements and the representations which accompanied them is such as to satisfy the Commissioner that the aggregate given above, namely $243,000,000 of stocks and bonds, is not an over estimate.

Miscellaneous Securities (Partially Known and Partially Estimated).

Municipal bonds	$ 7,500,000
Canal bonds	5,063,967
Mining shares and bonds	10,000,000
A careful estimate of other forms of foreign indebtedness on November 1, 1869, gives the following additional elements:	
Capital lying in the United States in consequence of the comparatively low rate of interest in Europe—credits, bills of exchange, etc.	50,000,000
Cuban moneys temporarily transferred in consequence of the revolution	25,000,000
Foreign capital invested in mortgages of real estate, etc.	25,000,000

Recapitulation.

State bonds	$100,000,000
Railway bonds	130,000,000
Railway shares	113,000,000
Mining bonds and shares	10,000,000
Municipal bonds	7,500,000
Miscellaneous bonds and shares	5,000,000
Capital temporarily invested	50,000,000
Cuban moneys	25,000,000
Real estate mortgages, etc.	25,000,000
Total	$465,500,000

Adding $1,000,000,000 of federal securities held abroad, as before estimated, we have, as the total of the present foreign indebtedness of the United States, the sum of $1,465,500,000; on which, at an average of 6 per cent., an annual payment of interest accrues to the amount of $87,930,000; and of which $80,000,000 may be estimated as paid regularly.

Adverse Foreign Balance for 1868-'69

But enormous as is this sum, the process of incurring indebtedness still continues as actively as ever. The account of the United States with foreign countries for the fiscal year ending June 30, 1869, may be exhibited substantially as follows:

Imports of merchandise, gold value		$417,371,765
Exports (gold values)	$275,611,591	
Re-exports, etc.	10,907,753	
		286,519,344
		130,852,421
Less excess of foreign goods, in bond, 1869 over 1868		14,702,079
Adverse balance 1868-'9 merchandise account		116,150,342

Movement of Specie and Bullion.

Exports	$ 42,915,966
Re-exports	14,222,414
Total	57,138,380
Imports	19,654,776
Loss of specie and bullion	37,483,604

If we suppose the excess of specie and bullion exports to have been devoted exclusively to the liquidation of. balances incurred on the merchandise account, the remaining balance on this account to be settled for in some other manner would be $78,666,738.

To this sum must be added the following other items:

Obligations for interest (paid), estimated	$80,000,000
Excess of freights carried in foreign bottoms[1]	24,000,000
Expenditures of Americans in foreign countries[1]	25,000,000

Assuming that the sums chargeable to smuggling and undervaluation of imports are counterbalanced by the undervaluation of exports,[2] the sum total of the adverse balance of indebtedness of the United States to foreign countries will, at the present time, probably average about $210,000,000 per annum.

To meet and settle this constantly increasing and adverse balance there would seem to be, under the present condition of prices and cost of production in the United States, but one resource, viz: to remit certificates of indebtedness—national, State or corporate.

[1] Long footnotes show the method by which these estimates were obtained.

[2] If we confine ourselves to the comparison of the values given to imports and exports, respectively, in previous years, this may be considered a reasonable estimate; but for the last fiscal year it is certainly not the case. Under the present organization of the Bureau of Statistics, the values given to the exports of the country have been scrutinized and verified to such an extent as to leave but little doubt that the statement for the last year is substantially accurate and complete. The fraudulent undervaluation of imports, however, it is not within the power of such an agency to prevent.

And this process is undoubtedly adopted, and goes on, month after month and year after year, without occasioning thus far any marked disturbance in the trade and commerce of the country.

Now, whether so great an exchange of evidences of indebtedness for foreign commodities or foreign services is advantageous to the country at large, or how long such a method of liquidating balances can continue, are questions which it is not necessary to immediately consider, inasmuch as we would rather direct attention at this point to the fact that, while before the war we were able to wholly pay for our foreign imports and services with the products of our own industry, including, after the discovery of California, and up to the beginning of the war, such a proportion only of our product of gold as it would have been practically useless and even mischievous for us to retain, we are not now so doing; and this latter circumstance would seem to prove beyond question that the aggregate of national production does not maintain the same proportion as formerly to the aggregate of national consumption.

It must not be forgotten, furthermore, that by the remittance of bonds we have simply deferred payment, and must hereafter export products to meet these obligations; and whenever such export of products in payment for past imports shall be made, it will of necessity be in addition to the export then made to pay for current imports. Product for product is the absolute condition on which alone commerce is possible.

IV. A Partial Income Account for Great Britain

In drawing up the income account for Great Britain—and, for that matter, for most of the countries of Europe—it is necessary to take account of the fact that imports are valued c.i.f.; exports, f.o.b. The official figures for imports, therefore, overstate the amount which Great Britain must pay to foreigners for goods imported; for a large share of the carrying, insurance, and commission charges included as part of the cost of the goods is not a charge paid to foreigners, but is paid to British shipowners, British insurance companies, and British commission houses. One of the earliest British studies to point

this out quite clearly was that of A. D. McKay, in an open letter published by the *Economist,* December 8, 1877, in which he replied to an earlier open letter in the same paper by a Mr. Rathbone.[6] McKay's purpose was to disprove Rathbone's statement to the effect that Britain's excess of imports over exports was requiring a sacrifice of British-owned foreign investments. It is interesting to notice the way in which this purpose determined the form and content of the account which he presented. All classes of income or outgo directly pertaining to commodity trade are included in the account. Other items are omitted or are given somewhat casual notice. For example, some interesting information is given concerning British investments abroad, but no attempt is made to estimate the total income of the country from this source. McKay's letter with the exception of the introductory and closing paragraphs is given below.

EXCERPTS FROM MCKAY'S LETTER TO THE "ECONOMIST" *

The materials on which I shall chiefly depend will be the Board of Trade Returns, but as it will be desirable to refer to a period for which the figures are most complete, I shall fall back upon the twenty-first report of the Commissioners of her Majesty's Customs, and I shall take the total imports and exports therein specified for the nineteen years, embracing 1858 and 1876. Any change in imports or exports for any given year cannot be of sufficient specific importance, I therefore propose to view the finances of the nineteen years together. The total amounts then, including bullion imported and exported, from 1858 to 1876, were:

	£
Imports	5,986,630,795
Exports	4,793,122,362
Excess Imports	1,193,508,433

[6] The London *Economist,* 1877, pp. 1394-1396; 1458-9; 1522; 1555. See discussion of this study in Chapter II, pp. 20-22.

* The London *Economist,* 1877, p. 1459.

Taking the merchandise apart from the bullion, the figures stand thus—

	Merchandise	Bullion
	£	£
Imports	5,432,497,611	554,133,184
Exports	4,332,941,318	460,181,044
Excess	1,099,556,293	93,952,140

Taking the reading adopted by Mr. Rathbone, I shall proceed on the ground that "the value of imports by the Board of Trade is based on the prices of articles current in this country at the time of arrival," subject to "deduction of freight charges and profits due to British shipowners and merchants."

The series of items to be deducted from imports are:

	£
Buyers' discount, ranging from 1¼ per cent. to 2½, but averaging, on a moderate estimate, 1¾ per cent., on 5,432,497,611 *l*	95,068,708
Freights in British bottoms—1858 to 1874, 149,870,592 tons, at 30s	224,805,888
Ditto, 1875 to 1876, 26,521,663 tons, at 20s	26,521,663
Marine insurance on three-fourths of the total imports, allowing one-fourth to be covered in foreign offices—three-fourths, 4,489,973,097 *l;* add 10 per cent., 448,997,309 *l;* together, 4,938,970,406 *l,* at 15s per cent.............	37,042,278
Sundry charges on imports goods, consisting of dues, wharfage, cartage, porterage, and other receiving and warehousing expenses, 266,061,298 tons, at 3s per ton	39,909,194
Foreign bill stamps on imports goods, 5,432,497,611 *l,* at 2s per cent.	5,432,497
Bankers' commission on same, at 2s 6d per cent..........	6,790,622
Commission and brokerage on same, 1½ per cent.........	81,487,464
Freight on imports bullion, 554,133,184 *l,* at 5s per cent....	1,385,332
Total charges on imports	518,443,846

To be added to exports—

	£
Freights in British bottoms—1858 to 1874, 167,642,892 tons, at 30s	251,464,338
Ditto, 1875 to 1876, 29,649,887 tons, at 20s	29,649,887

Marine insurance on total exports, 4,793,122,362 *l;* add 10 per cent., 479,312,236 *l;* together, 5,272,434,598 *l,* at 15s per cent.	39,543,259
Bankers' commission on exports—goods, 4,332,941,318 *l,* at 2s 6d per cent.	5,416,178
Six months' interest on same at 5s per cent.	109,323,532
Profit on same at 5s per cent.	216,647,064
Freight on exports bullion, 460,181,044 *l,* at 5s per cent.	1,150,452
Total charges on exports	652,194,710

With deductions and additions, the total imports and exports will stand thus:

	£		£
Imports	5,986,639,795	Exports	4,793,122,362
Deduct	518,443,646	Add	652,194,710
	5,468,187,146		5,445,317,072
		Net apparent balance against us..	22,870,077
	5,468,187,149		5,468,187,149

It will thus be seen that by a fair estimate of ordinary charges, and such profits as the business experience of the past nineteen years will consider to be within the mark, the total balance apparently against us is only about *twenty-three millions,* or a little more than a million per annum. But we have now to see how the balance will tend if we introduce the vast sums that must constantly be coming due in the shape of interest on foreign and colonial Government loans, foreign and colonial railways, plantations, and a myriad of miscellaneous investments, which (even deducting defaulters) are paying remunerative dividends. Our Government guaranteed investments in India, held in this country, cannot be much less than two hundred millions, paying, at least, four and a half per cent. Of Australian loans we hold, probably, over forty millions, paying over five per cent. Of Canadian loans, we hold about 20 millions, averaging 4½ per cent. In addition to this, we are the owners of no small sum in colonial and foreign railways, and miscellaneous enterprises; and to crown the whole it is more

than probable that we have a good share in every national debt in the world. Keeping these items in view, it must be obvious that, however great our imports may be, they may reasonably be accounted for with more satisfaction than concern. The profits of our foreign and colonial trade, and the interest arising from our foreign and colonial investments, will only be partially consumed. A large portion will fall to be invested either abroad or at home, and unless foreign investments are more attractive, we may expect the amount to augment our imports to a greater extent than hitherto, without any danger of our trenching upon capital.

While I agree with Mr. Rathbone as to the evil of extravagance, I must say that I have not yet encountered any evidence to substantiate the charge against us as a nation, that we spend what we cannot afford. . . .

A. D. McKay.

Liverpool, 1st December, 1877.

V. Canada's Income Account and Foreign Debt

The following excerpts from Coats' Cost of Living Study for Canada [7] shows the peculiar form of account which he adopted, and the line of reasoning by which he arrived at this form of presentation.

EXCERPTS FROM COATS' STUDY *

All international trade is, of course, of the nature of barter. Canada pays her foreign indebtedness with goods, and similarly receives payments from abroad in goods. Speaking for exports first, it may be held from the present standpoint that they represent broadly two classes of payments, the first being remittances on obligations of various kinds owed abroad, and the second being payments for goods purchased. Total imports may be similarly divided, namely first, into the goods which represent payments by foreign nations on obligations in Canada, and second, the goods coming in exchange for the second class of exports above. Now, when the value of these incoming goods is found to be in excess of the exports sent in payment, that excess must clearly represent

[7] See discussion of this study, Chapter II, pp. 27-28.

* *Report of the Canadian Board of Inquiry into the Cost of Living in Canada,* Vol. II, pp. 890 and 906.

a loan to Canada by other countries, and the sum of these annual excesses must be considered as a close approximation of the amount of capital which Canada has been borrowing abroad in the period under review.

To make such a calculation, however, the amounts having to do with the exchange of "invisible" goods must be separate from our figures of foreign trade. The items which must be deducted from the total export figures are the following: (1) payments of interest and sinking fund sent abroad; (2) payments of dividends on Canadian securities held abroad; (3) remittances of immigrant residents; (4) expenditures of Canadian travellers, students, etc., abroad; (5) the export of capital which accompanies emigration; (6) net payments to foreign insurance companies; (7) payments to foreign ships and railroads engaged in the handling of goods for Canada, and (8) Canadian capital sent abroad for investment.

To be deducted from total imports are the following items: (1) capital brought into the country by immigrants, including Chinese head-tax; (2) earnings on Canadian capital invested in other countries, including call loans in New York; (3) expenditures in Canada of travellers from other countries; (4) remittances to Canada by friends of residents; (5) insurance payments to Canada, and (6) earnings of Canadian ships engaged in foreign commerce.

We will now proceed to estimate the amounts involved for the period 1900-1914 under each of the above headings. This completed, the result will be applied to the export and import trade totals respectively, when a final calculation ought to reveal fairly accurately the net amount of capital which Canada has borrowed abroad since 1900.

The Trade Balance, 1900-1914

(1) Exports		$4,031,400,000	
Deductions from Exports:			
Interest	$1,488,000,000		
Remittances to friends	150,000,000		
Tourist expenditures	150,000,000		
Emigrant expenditures	245,000,000		
Insurance payments	117,000,000		
Freight	60,000,000		
Call money outside Canada	35,000,000		
		2,245,000,000	
Excess of exports over deductions			$1,786,400,000

(2) Imports		$5,359,700,000	
Deductions from Imports:			
Receipts from immigration	$ 650,000,000		
Tourists in Canada	140,000,000		
Remittances to friends ..	50,000,000		
Insurance payments to Canada	20,000,000	860,000,000	
Excess of imports over deductions..			$4,499,700,000
Balance representing borrowings ..			2,713,300,000

VI. Britain's Income Account and Foreign Investments

C. K. Hobson, in his *Export of Capital,* furnishes an interesting example of the way in which the income account of a country may be used in estimating the country's foreign investments. The following excerpts from his summary tables will indicate the form, content, and method of his work on the accounts.

He first estimates the international income and outgo of the country from all sources except from interest and dividends. The net figure thus obtained must, of course, represent the net income of the country from foreign investments, plus the net outgo of the country for investments abroad. The first of the two excerpts given below is from his table summarizing these data for the whole period 1870-1912.

HOBSON'S ESTIMATES OF NET CAPITAL AND INTEREST TRANSACTIONS.*

(Figures in Millions Sterling)

Year	Shipping Earnings, etc.	Commission Insurance and Banking Charges	Government Services, Remittance, and Old Ships	New Ships	Total of Columns 1, 2, 3, 4	Excess of Imports	Balance of Capital and Interest Transactions
1870	39.5	11.0	6.0	1	57.5	69.8	+ 12.3
1871	50	12.0	6.2	1	69.2	51.7	— 17.5
1872	51	15.5	6.4	2	74.9	39.4	— 35.5
1910	95	26.7	14.0	8.7	144.4	159.6	+ 15.2
1911	110	26.3	14.2	5.7	156.1	134.9	— 21.2
1912	156[a]	29.9	14.4	7.0	207.3[a]	157.3	— 50.0

* Hobson, C. K., *Export of Capital,* p. 197.

[a] These figures are probably excessive.

He then proceeds to a calculation of the two component parts making up the balancing item in the table above. On the basis of Sir George Paish's estimate of Britain's income from foreign investments in 1907, together with the reports of the Inland Revenue Commission, he estimates the income of the country from foreign investments for each of the years in question. Having thus found one of the two items entering into the above "balance," he finds the other by algebraic subtraction. The excerpt below will show his presentation of this final step in the calculation.

HOBSON'S ESTIMATES OF NEW INVESTMENTS ABROAD *

(Figures in Millions Sterling)

Year	Estimated Income from Abroad	Balance of Capital and Interest Transactions	Export of Capital
1870	44.0[a]	+ 12.3	31.7
1871	46.0[a]	− 17.5	63.5
1872	48.0[a]	− 35.5	83.5
1910	166.0	+ 15.2	150.8
1911	171.0[a]	− 21.2	192.2
1912	176.0[a]	− 50.0	226.0[b]

* *ibid.*, p. 204.

[a] These figures are assumed. [b] This figure is probably excessive.

VII. A *Mixed* "Balance Sheet"

It will be seen that the "international trade balance sheet" given below [8] includes both capital items and income and outgo items. Except for the fact that the years 1865-1873 have been omitted from the excerpt given, it represents an exact reproduction of the summary table published by Frank D. Graham in his article "International Trade Under Depreciated Paper, The United States, 1862-79."

[8] See discussion of this point in Chapter V, pp. 59-60.

EXCERPT FROM GRAHAM'S SUMMARY TABLE *

International Trade Balance Sheet (Specie Values in Thousands of Dollars)[1]

United States in Account with Foreign Nations

Dr. Cr.

Year Ending June 30	Merchandise imports	Gold and silver specie and bullion imports	Freights payable	Net interest payments	Repayments on loans	Total debits	Merchandise exports	Gold and silver specie and bullion exports	Freights receivable	Sales of ships	Loans floated	Total credits
1860	$353,616	$ 8,550	$13,400	$18,000	......	$393,566	$333,575	$ 66,545	$27,908	......	$15,000	$443,028
1861	289,310	46,339	13,410	18,000	......	367,059	219,553	29,790	17,997	......	10,000	277,340
1862	189,356	16,415	11,349	15,000	$ 25,000	257,120	190,670	36,886	12,418	$4,710	......	244,684
1863	243,335	9,584	14,317	12,000	25,000	304,236	203,963	64,156	9,860	8,885	......	286,864
1864	316,447	13,115	24,835	15,000	......	369,397	158,837	105,395	6,724	12,034	80,000	362,990
1874	567,406	28,454	40,532	60,000	......	696,392	586,282	66,629	15,713	......	51,000	719,624
1875	533,005	20,900	38,294	63,000	......	655,199	513,442	92,132	13,962	......	20,200	649,736
1876	460,741	15,936	32,113	60,000	50,000	618,790	540,384	56,505	14,839	......	......	611,728
1877	451,323	40,774	32,956	55,000	100,000	680,053	602,474	56,161	15,404	......	......	674,039
1878	437,051	38,437	30,749	45,000	150,000	701,237	694,865	33,739	16,318	......	......	744,922
Grand Total...........						$10,082,910						$9,981,099

* *Quarterly Journal of Economics*, 1922, p. 231.

[1] This balance sheet, the basis of the study, was prepared after a comprehensive examination of sources. All figures are **in gold values. Paper prices, where they occurred in the statistics, were reduced to their gold equivalents at the rate** of premium on gold prevailing at the period which the quotation covers. Quotations of merchandise and of specie and bullion exports and imports are based on government statistics, and the figures on sales of ships are derived from government **reports. All other figures are estimates** computed from unofficial sources such as the *Commercial and Financial Chronicle, Bankers' Magazine, London Economist*. Each set of figures **has been determined** quite independently of any other.

APPENDIX B

QUESTIONNAIRE ON CAPITAL TRANSACTIONS

USED BY THE UNITED STATES DEPARTMENT OF COMMERCE[1]

One of the three accounts which make up the international financial statement discussed in Chapter V and illustrated in Chapter VII is the statement of current capital transactions. As we have said in the discussion of the data, Chapter VIII, there was little done in the way of collecting this class of information until after the war. And in some countries, very little has thus far been done along this line. For this reason it may prove of interest to present the questionnaire used in the collection of these data for the United States, and to outline briefly the way in which it has been developed.

The questionnaire which the United States Department of Commerce has used for securing information with regard to deposits with foreigners, loans and advances to foreigners, and short-term investments placed abroad by American bankers, and with regard to corresponding items placed here by foreigners, is the result of some eight years of experience with the question. For its beginning it dates back to the study which Dr. John H. Williams published in the *Review of Economic Statistics* covering the accounts for the year 1920. In the questionnaire for that year Dr. Williams limited his inquiry

[1] With the exception of the introductory paragraph, this appendix was prepared by Grosvenor M. Jones, Chief of the Finance and Investment Division of the United States Department of Commerce.

to the movement of securities issued abroad and sold here, and of American securities formerly held abroad but returned to this side. The results which he obtained proved far from satisfactory. In referring to the subject a year later he said: "A questionnaire which we sent to leading financial houses last year concerning dealings in 1920 brought important results in only a few instances." [2]

In his study for 1921 Dr. Williams made use of the results of questionnaires distributed by a leading New York bank to "the principal domestic banks, private bankers, and foreign banks, of New York, two large banks of Boston, and the more representative members of the American Manufacturers Export Association, and the Exporters and Importers Association, asking them to report the status of their balances with foreign countries." [3] A questionnaire sent to trading concerns sought information as of July 1, 1920, and July 1, 1921, on "all used credit extended, uncollected items and accounts whether due or to mature, balances in foreign banks, holdings of exchange and short-time foreign securities" and the *per contra* items. The questionnaire to banks and bankers was somewhat similar but requested the inclusion of all such items, whether for their own account, or discounted, or taken for collection. The banks were also asked to report their holdings of foreign-drawn dollar bills as of the beginning and end of the year covered. With regard to the results obtained Dr. Williams says: "This year a questionnaire sent out by a leading New York bank has yielded much better results than have ever before been available on these items; and these results we are now permitted to make public for the first time. The questionnaire was distributed to 41 leading banks and financial houses handling securities of these kinds, of which 26 reported their dealings in

[2] *The Review of Economic Statistics,* July, 1922 (Preliminary Vol. IV, No. 3), p. 205. The questionnaires used in this inquiry are reproduced in the appendix to the report. *ibid.,* p. 214.

[3] *ibid.,* p. 208.

1919, 1920, and 1921, the remaining 15 replying but giving no figures." [4]

During these earlier years of the post-war period there was much discussion among economists of the probable effects of the collapse of the post-war boom in our export trade. All were agreed that a considerable deduction from the official figures for commodity exports should be made to cover losses from bad debts, etc. But as to how large the deduction should be, there was no such agreement. Accordingly the principal questionnaire used by Dr. Williams was that sent to trading concerns—largely on the subject of accumulated balances due from abroad on merchandise transactions. The somewhat similar questionnaire sent to bankers covered the same ground, and probably elicited duplicatory data, but in addition it called for information concerning ordinary banking balances. A special questionnaire to banks and bankers on the international movement of securities was also used for the year 1921, as indicated by the quotations cited above from Dr. Williams' report for that year. It is doubtful, however, whether the returns for the 26 banks reporting even approximately covered the volume of such transactions.

In the first study undertaken by the Department of Commerce, that for the year 1922, Dr. Williams was a collaborator. The questionnaires used were very similar to those which he had adopted the year previous, and again the chief stress was on the "unfunded credit balance" arising from export trade transactions. There was a far wider distribution of these questionnaires than before.

For the report for 1923, no questionnaire was sent to merchants and manufacturers, "as it seemed certain that the unfunded credit balance would show a further decline but probably so slight that the results of a questionnaire would neither be correct nor enlightening." [5] On the other hand,

[4] *ibid.*, p. 205.

[5] *Trade Information Bulletin* 215, p. 16.

greater stress was laid on the questionnaire relating to foreigners' bank deposits here and American deposits abroad, as well as upon the inquiry regarding international movement of securities. The number of items in the questionnaire was increased, and the questions were made more specific. An effort was also made to secure returns from a larger number of banks and bankers and this effort resulted in fuller and more accurate returns. As in previous years, the Federal Reserve Bank of New York was used as medium for securing the data.

In the following year the Department of Commerce took over the task of distributing the questionnaire to bankers, and acting upon the suggestion that fuller data could be had if a number of the inquiries were combined, the questionnaire was considerably compressed. At the same time an effort was made to secure returns from the principal banks in all of the leading cities instead of limiting the field of inquiry almost entirely to banks and bankers within the jurisdiction of the Federal Reserve Bank of New York. The result was that in the study for 1924 a country-wide compilation was made for the first time, but the information secured lacked some of the definiteness that characterized the returns for 1923.

Accordingly, the questionnaire for 1925 was slightly amplified. Again a country-wide survey was made, although the returns for banks outside the largest cities did not affect the net result in any important degree.

For the study now in progress, covering the year 1926, the questionnaire has been made more specific than in any previous year. This action was decided upon at the urgent request of several leading banking authorities who felt that in the present phase of international finance it is important to have fuller and more detailed information concerning the transactions bearing on our current financial status. The questionnaire was drawn up after consulting with a group consisting of an official of the Federal Reserve Bank of New York and representatives of

several leading banks and banking houses of New York. It is believed that in its present form the questionnaire is the best that has been used to date, and if adhered to should produce comparable data of great practical value not only to theoretical economists but also to the bankers themselves.

The form of the banking questionnaire used in the study for 1926 is given below.

January 31, 1927.

Questionnaire to International Banks and Bankers

(This questionnaire was prepared in collaboration with the Federal Reserve Bank of New York in order to avoid duplication.)

Please return to Grosvenor M. Jones, Chief, Finance and Investment Division, Department of Commerce, Washington, D. C.

I. OLD CAPITAL SECURITIES TRANSFERRED INTERNATIONALLY.

Question 1.—Please estimate the total amounts of hitherto American-held capital securities which, through you, WERE SOLD TO FOREIGNERS, during the calendar year 1926.

(a) American stocks and bonds sold abroad $........

(b) Foreign stocks and bonds sold abroad $........

Question 2.—Please estimate the total amounts of hitherto foreign-held capital securities which, through you, WERE BOUGHT BY AMERICANS during the calendar year 1926.

(c) American stocks and bonds re-bought from abroad .... $........

(d) *Foreign stocks and bonds bought from abroad .... $........

*Note: Item "d" does not include your public offerings in the United States of foreign stocks and bonds.

Question 3.—Please state the aggregate market value in dollars of stocks and bonds held by you for account of foreigners * as follows:

(e) As of close of business December 31, 1925 .... $........

(f) As of close of business December 31, 1926 .... $........

Question 4.—Please state the aggregate market value in dollars of stocks and bonds held abroad for your own or your American customers' account as follows:

(g) As of close of business December 31, 1925 .... $........

(h) As of close of business December 31, 1926 .... $........

II. "UNFUNDED" ITEMS OF INDEBTEDNESS.

Please indicate in the blanks below, how much your institution owed foreigners,* and how much foreigners* owed your institution at the beginning and end of 1926 on account of "unfunded" items.

1. *Deposits, Loans, etc., Due from Foreigners**

A. Total deposits (both time and demand) with foreigners:*

1. As of close of business December 31, 1925 .... $........
2. As of close of business December 31, 1926 .... $........

B. Total loans and advances (including overdrafts) to by foreigners:*

1. As of close of business December 31, 1925 .... $........
2. As of close of business December 31, 1926 .... $........

C. Short-term investments made abroad by foreigners* for your own or your customers' account (including all bills and short-term securities as well as loans placed abroad for your own or your customers' account):

1. As of close of business December 31, 1925 .... $........
2. As of close of business December 31, 1926 .... $........

2. *Deposits, Loans, etc., Due to Foreigners**

D. Total deposits (both time and demand) of foreigners* with you:

1. As of close of business December 31, 1925 .... $........
2. As of close of business December 31, 1926 .... $........

E. Total loans and advances (including overdrafts) to you by foreigners *:
1. As of close of business December 31, 1925 .... $........
2. As of close of business December 31, 1926 .... $........

F. Short-term investments made by you for account of foreigners * (including all bills and short-term Treasury securities purchased by you and held for their account, also call and time loans placed by you for their account):
1. As of close of business December 31, 1925 .... $........
2. As of close of business December 31, 1926 .... $........

* Note: Please interpret the term "foreigners" as including:
1. Foreign governments, banks, bankers, and others resident abroad; and
2. Foreign branches of American banks.

Signed ....
Name of Institution ....
City ....

INDEX

ROUTLEDGE LIBRARY EDITIONS:
ACCOUNTING

Volume 52

THE INTERNATIONAL ACCOUNTS